IS-331: Introduction to Radiological Emergency Preparedness (REP)

By

Fema

10/31/2013

Lesson 1: REP Basics

Lesson Overview

This lesson presents basic Radiological Emergency Preparedness (REP) concepts.

Lesson Objectives

At the completion of this lesson, you will be able to:

- Define the four Emergency Classification Levels (ECLs).
- Define Protective Action Guides (PAGs) and select examples of protective actions.
- Define Emergency Planning Zone.

REP and ECLs

FEMA, which has been incorporated into the U.S. Department of Homeland Security, is the lead Federal agency for planning and preparedness for all types of peacetime radiological emergencies. In this course, we'll focus on incidents at nuclear facilities.

Responsibility for planning and preparedness activities within and outside the nuclear power plant boundaries is divided between the U.S. Nuclear Regulatory Commission (NRC) and FEMA.

Radiological Emergency Preparedness

NRC is responsible for "onsite" activities—those that take place at the power plant. FEMA is responsible for "offsite" activities—State and local government emergency preparedness activities that take place beyond the plant boundaries. Within this role, FEMA:

- Reviews and evaluates offsite radiological emergency response plans (RERPs) developed by State and local governments.
- Evaluates radiological emergency planning (REP) exercises conducted by State and local governments to determine whether their RERPs can be implemented.
- Reports to the NRC on the adequacy of offsite emergency planning and preparedness.
- Coordinates the activities of Federal agencies involved in the radiological emergency planning process.

REP exercises are designed to test the capability of offsite response organizations (OROs) to protect public health and safety through the implementation of their RERPs under simulated conditions.

FEMA's evaluation of REP exercises is an important element in ensuring State and local jurisdictions' readiness for radiological emergencies.

Nuclear Facilities

In September 2002, 104 commercial nuclear power reactors were licensed to operate in the U.S. Those nuclear facilities are:

- Located in 31 states.
- Spread through the eastern half of the country, with a few in the West.

Effective emergency response depends on grading the level of emergency and then responding accordingly. Emergency Classification Levels (ECLs) were developed for this purpose.

Emergency Classification Levels

Emergency Classification Levels (ECLs) stem from Emergency Action Levels (EALs). An EAL is an
onsite observable measure that a nuclear facility uses to determine how and when it should notify
the offsite emergency response organizations. Each nuclear power utility establishes its own
specific conditions or instrumentation readings—according to guidelines set by the NRC—that will
initiate a particular EAL.

The Four ECLs

When an EAL is initiated, it triggers the utility to declare the corresponding ECL. There are four Emergency Classification Levels:

Notification of Unusual Event (NOUE)

NOUEthe lowest emergency level—can be triggered by any problem within the plant that could potentially lead to a degradation in the level of safety. No release of radioactive material is expected at the time of the event, although conditions could deteriorate in the future. Because no release is expected, offsite emergency workers should not have to monitor for a release. Remember, though—an event can begin as a NOUE and then escalate.

Alert

Alert is the second lowest emergency level. The difference between an Alert and a NOUE is that a release may be possible under an alert. However, such a release is expected to be small and limited to a fraction of the EPA Protective Action Guides (PAGs). (We'll learn more about PAGs later in this lesson.) An event can escalate from the Alert level if safety conditions deteriorate further, or it can deescalate.

Site Area Emergency (SAE)

An SAE indicates a serious safety condition at the plant. With this type of event:

- Major safety systems have failed or are about to fail.
- A release is possible but is not expected to exceed EPA Protective Action Guides (PAGs), except at the site boundary.
- Plant conditions are such that radiation levels within the plant boundaries could exceed the PAGs.

General Emergency (GE)

GE is the highest emergency level. In this type of event:

- The core would be either damaged or expected to become damaged.
- A release could be imminent and could exceed Environmental Protection Agency (EPA) PAGs. However, there could be a General Emergency without a release occurring.

Plants in the U.S. were designed to ensure core integrity. A plant whose core becomes damaged may be operating outside its design specifications, and operators might not know how to fix the problem.

Event Frequency

Unusual events of the four types just described are relatively rare in the U.S. The more serious the event, the more rare its occurrence. The following chart shows how many events of each type have occurred over a recent 5-year period and overall since 1989.

Classification of Events Under Reactor Licensee Emergency Plans						
Event / Year	1997	1998	1999	2000	2001	1989-2001
NOUE	40	26	34	18	13	1174
Alert	3	4	4	1	3	89
SAE	0	0	0	0	0	5
GE	0	0	0	0	0	0

Protective Actions

One of the distinctions between the various ECLs relates to whether Protective Action Guides (PAGs) are likely to be exceeded.

What Are Protective Actions?

In responding to radiological emergencies, public officials are faced with making decisions and taking actions to protect the public from the potentially damaging effects of radiation. A ***protective action*** is an action taken to avoid or reduce the radiation dose when the benefits are sufficient to offset any undesirable features of the protective action. Protective actions can be taken to fulfill several different objectives, including:

- To remove or keep people from the area where exposure to radiation could occur.
- To shield people from the radioactive release.
- To limit the damage caused by a certain type of radiation exposure.
- To limit the amount of radioactive material ingested through food.

Examples of protective actions include:

- Evacuation
- Sheltering
- Access control
- Use of potassium iodide (KI)
- Use of stored feed and protected water for animals
- Condemnation of food supplies
- Relocation
- Decontamination
- Plant Conditions

OROs use the best information available at the time of an incident to make decisions about protective actions. The urgency with which decisions must be made can vary greatly, depending on situational factors such as the ECL and how quickly the event is unfolding.

Time Factors

It appears to take a minimum of about a half-hour from the initiating event before a release could occur, as indicated in the following table. Response time must be fast enough to react within this time if necessary.

Time Factors Associated with Release

Time from initiating event to start of atmospheric release	0.5 to several hours
Period during which radioactive material may be continuously released	0.5 hours to several days
Time at which the major portion of a release may occur	0.5 hours to 1 day after start of release
Time for release to reach exposure points:	

. . . at site boundary minutes

. . . at 5 miles 0.5 to 2 hours

. . . at 10 miles 1 to 4 hours

Protective Action Guides

In 1991, the U.S. Environmental Protection Agency (EPA) published the *Manual of Protective Action Guides and Protective Actions for Nuclear Incidents*. The manual assists public officials in planning for emergency response to nuclear emergencies within the required timeframe.

A ***Protective Action Guide (PAG)*** is the projected dose to individuals in the population that warrants taking protective action. Projected dose means the dose that would be received if no protective actions were taken.

A PAG answers the question, "What level of likely radiation exposure would warrant our taking this particular protective action (for example, evacuation)."

Considering the Risks

PAGs are established to minimize health risks, both immediate and delayed. They have two broad goals: to avoid **immediate** health risks and to keep the risk of **delayed** health effects within upper bounds that adequately protect public health under emergency conditions and that are reasonably achievable.

PAGs do not imply an acceptable level of risk. They also do not represent a boundary between safe and unsafe conditions. Rather, PAGs are the approximate levels at which the associated protective actions are justified. PAGs are used only in an effort to minimize the risk from an event that is occurring or has already occurred.

Nuclear Incident Phases

Protective Action Guides are tied to the time elapsed since the incident began. Nuclear incidents have three phases, which are linear but may overlap:

- The **early phase** (or emergency phase) begins at the start of a nuclear incident when protective actions are required. It ends when the source and release have been brought under control. This phase can last from hours to days.
- The **intermediate phase** begins when the source and the release have been brought under control and ends when protective actions have been terminated. For dose projection, this phase is assumed to last a year.
- The **late phase** (or recovery phase) encompasses the recovery actions designed to reduce radiation levels in the environment to acceptable levels for unrestricted use. It begins when protective actions have ended and may extend from months to years.

PAGs for the Early Phase

For the early phase, the PAGs are based on the total amount of radiation received from two sources:

- External radiation exposure (e.g., groundshine and cloudshine).
    - Internal radiation exposure, from inhalation. This type of radiation continues to affect the internal organs once it is inside the body.
    - In the early phase, the time available to implement the most effective protective actions may be limited. As soon as an incident is known to have occurred, a preliminary evaluation is made to gain information that will enable decisionmakers to decide on the best protective actions. The preliminary evaluation may reveal such information as:
- Nature and potential magnitude of the incident.
- Likelihood of a major release.
- Characteristics of the situation, such as potential exposure pathways, populations at risk, and projected doses.

PAGs of 1 to 5 REM have been established for the early phase, as shown in the table below.

PAG	Comments
1- 5 REM*	Evacuation (or, for some situations, sheltering). • Evacuation should normally be initiated at 1 REM. • No specific minimum level is set for initiating sheltering. In some cases, sheltering should be considered at projected doses below 1 REM. • Sheltering may be preferred when it provides equal or greater protection. • Sheltering should always be used when evacuation is not carried out at projected doses of 1 REM or more.

* Committed dose equivalent to the thyroid may be 5 times larger; committed dose equivalent to the skin may be 50 times larger. See the glossary for REM and similar terms.

Other Early Phase PAGs

In addition to these general PAGs, specific PAGs for the early phase have been developed for emergency workers, use of potassium iodide, and ingestion levels.

Emergency Workers PAGs

The dose limits for emergency workers are higher than for the general public, for two reasons:

- Emergency workers may need to take more risks (i.e., receive a higher dose) in order to aid the general public.
- Emergency workers usually have potassium iodide and dosimetry to help mitigate this additional risk.

The dose limits for this group vary from 5 to 25 rem according to the importance of the task being performed. At doses over 25 rem, emergency workers must be made fully aware of the risks involved and may continue to work only on a voluntary basis.

Emergency Worker Dose Limits		
Dose Limit REM	**Activity**	**Condition**
5	All	
10	Protecting valuable property	Lower dose not practicable
25	Life saving, protection of large populations	Lower dose not practicable
>25	Life saving, protection of large populations	Only on a voluntary basis to persons fully aware of the risks involved

Use of Potassium Iodide

Exposure to radioactive iodine poses a long-term risk of thyroid cancer. Potassium iodide (KI) can safely be used to block the thyroid's uptake of radioiodines. Use of KI provides an important means of protection for certain groups, including:

- Institutionalized groups that cannot be evacuated.
- Emergency workers who must remain in the affected area to handle the emergency functions.
    - Members of the publicespecially children, who are highly vulnerable to thyroid cancer.
    - In 2002, the Federal policy on use of potassium iodide was revised as follows:
- KI should be stockpiled and distributed to emergency workers and institutionalized persons for radiological emergencies at a nuclear power plant.
- Use of KI should be considered for the general public within the 10-mile emergency-planning zone of a nuclear power plant.
- The decision on whether to use KI for the general public is left to the discretion of States and, in some cases, local governments.

Ingestion PAG

The ingestion PAG applies primarily to food and water. The ingestion PAG is 0.5 REM committed effective dose equivalent or 5 REM committed dose equivalent to an individual tissue or organ□ whichever is more limiting. The FDA recommends a combination of two approaches—Derived Intervention Levels (DILs) and protective actions—to limit the radiation dose received from consuming contaminated food.

DILs

DILs are limits on the radionuclide concentration permitted in food. DILs apply during the first year after a release.

Protective Actions

Protective actions are taken to reduce the amount of contamination. They are initiated immediately, subject to evaluation of the situation, and continue until concentrations (in the absence of the actions) remain below the DILs.

Ingestion Protective Actions

The protective actions for a specific incident are determined by the particulars of the situation. Once initiated, they continue at least until the concentrations are expected to remain below the DILs.

Prior to Confirmation of Contamination

Protective actions can be taken before the release or arrival of contamination if contamination of the environment is expected. The ECL (NOUE, Alert, SAE, and General Emergency) may be helpful for selecting appropriate measures. Appropriate actions prior to confirmation of contamination are likely to be confined to (1) simple precautionary actions to avoid or reduce the potential for contamination of food and animal feeds and (2) temporary embargoes to prevent the introduction into commerce of food which is likely to be contaminated. Examples include:

- Covering exposed products.
- Moving animals to shelter.
- Corralling livestock.
- Providing protected feed and water.

Foods Confirmed as Contaminated

Protective actions which should be implemented when the contamination in food equals or exceeds the DILs consist of (1) temporary embargoes to prevent the contaminated food from being introduced into commerce and (2) normal food production and processing actions that reduce the amount of contamination in or on food to below the DILs. Examples include:

- Holding food products to allow for radioactive decay.
- Removal of surface contamination by brushing, washing, or peeling.
- Avoiding blending contaminated food with uncontaminated food.
- More complex processing procedures to reduce contamination.

Animal Feeds Confirmed as Contaminated

Protective actions to reduce the impact of contamination in or on animal feeds (including pasture and water) are taken on a case-by-case basis. Examples include:

- Substituting uncontaminated water for contaminated water.
- Removing lactating dairy animals and meat animals from contaminated feeds and pasture.

- Substituting uncontaminated feed.
- Corralling livestock in an uncontaminated area.

PAGs for the Intermediate Phase

After the emergency has been brought under control, the focus shifts to protecting the public from whole body external exposure due to deposited material and inhalation of resuspended particulates. The major protective actions considered at this stage include:

- Relocation.
- Decontamination.
- Food and water restrictions.

In this phase the key issue is: What level of radiation should prompt a decision to relocate the population rather than allow them to live in the area that has been contaminated?

EPA advises simple dose reduction techniques if the projected dose is less than 2 REM for the first year, and relocation if the projected dose is greater than 2 REM for the first year.

Emergency Planning Zones

Emergency Planning Zones (EPZs) are generic areas around a nuclear facility for which planning is needed to ensure that prompt and effective actions can be taken to protect the public in the event of a nuclear incident.

EPZs are generic areas, not fixed distances or precise circles. The exact size and configuration of the EPZs surrounding a particular nuclear power facility are determined by State and local governments in consultation with FEMA and NRC. In establishing the size and shape of the EPZs, planners take local factors into account. Examples of planning factors include:

- Demography
- Topography
- Land characteristics
- Access routes
- Local jurisdiction boundaries

In reviewing emergency plans in your role as evaluator, you will see two different EPZs: the Plume EPZ and the Ingestion EPZ.

Plume EPZ

The plume EPZ is established for the short-term "plume exposure pathway." It is usually a 10-mile radius around the facility. This size of zone was selected because:

- Projected doses from design basis accidents and most core melt accidents would not exceed PAGs outside this zone.
- Worst-case melt accidents would not result in immediate life-threatening doses outside this zone.
- Detailed planning would provide a base for expanding response efforts, if necessary.

Plume phase exercises are evaluated by FEMA every 2 years.

Ingestion EPZ

The ingestion EPZ—designed for the longer-term "ingestion exposure pathway"—is usually a 50-mile radius around the nuclear facility and includes the plume EPZ. In this zone, the primary concern is radiological materials deposited on the ground and contaminating food and water. This size of the ingestion EPZ was chosen because:

- The likelihood of exceeding the ingestion pathway PAG levels at 50 miles is about the same as for exceeding the plume exposure pathway PAGs at 10 miles.
- Wind shifts during and after a release would limit the downwind range to 50 miles.
- Atmospheric iodine may convert to chemical forms that are not easily ingested.
- Most particulate material would be deposited on the ground within 50 miles.

Post-plume phase exercises are evaluated once every 6 years.

Lesson 2: Understanding Exercise Evaluation

Lesson Overview

This lesson introduces the regulatory basis, philosophy, and methodology of exercise evaluation and previews your role in the process.

Lesson Objectives

At the completion of this lesson, you will be able to:

- Explain how NUREG-0654 relates to REP plans.
- Describe the general philosophy governing REP evaluation.
- Identify the main elements of the evaluation methodology.
- Describe the overall role of the evaluator.

Regulatory Basis

Response Planning

Radiological Emergency Response Plans, developed by State and local governments, specify the actions to be taken during a nuclear plant incident. Offsite response activity during exercises is based on these plans. Each plan specifies what is to be done, how it is to be done, and by whom and when it is to be done

The regulatory basis for these plans is NUREG-0654/FEMA-REP-1, Criteria for Preparation and Evaluation of Radiological Emergency Response Plans and Preparedness in Support of Nuclear Power Plants. This guidance is the product of the joint FEMA/NRC Steering Committee.

NUREG-0654/FEMA-REP-1 describes planning standards that must be included in State and local plans. Emergency response plans do not have to follow a particular format, but they must contain certain material. Every REP plan must:

- Describe how each planning standard will be met.
- Have a table of contents.
- Define the facilities that will be used in the emergency response.
- Define the areas covered by the plan.
- Have a cross-reference to NUREG-0654/FEMA-REP-1.

The plans are the basis of the response and evaluator's need to be familiar with the plans/procedures for areas they evaluate.

Planning Standards

There are 15 planning standards (A and C through P) that apply to offsite operations. A sixteenth standard (B) applies to onsite response at the plant and is not addressed here. The 15 planning standards can be divided into two types: functional standards and supportive standards. Functional standards are tested during exercises. Supportive standards are not tested during exercises.

Functional Standards

Of the 15 standards, these 12 are functional standards, which are tested during exercises:

A. Assignment of Responsibility (Organizational Control)

C. Emergency Response Support and Resources

D. Emergency Classification System

E. Notification Methods and Procedures

F. Emergency Communication

G. Public Education and Information

H. Emergency Facilities and Equipment

I. Accident Assessment

J. Protective Response

K. Radiological Exposure Control

L. Medical and Public Health Support

M. Recovery and Reentry Planning and Post-Accident Operations

Supportive Standards

The 3 supportive standards, which are not tested during exercises, include:

N. Exercises and Drills

O. Radiological Emergency Response Training

P. Responsibility for the Planning Effort: Development, Periodic Review, and Distribution of Emergency Plans

The overall standard refers to assignment of responsibility for emergency response, but there are specific requirements within each standard. The plan must specify how it will meet each of the evaluation criteria.

Cross-Reference

Each REP plan must have a cross-reference between NUREG-0654/FEMA-REP-1 and the local plan's content. The cross-reference:

- Lists each planning standard.
- Indicates the page or section in the plan where that standard is addressed.

Exercising Emergency Response Plans

EMA, through the REP program, evaluates exercises to assess the capability of Offsite Response Organizations (OROs) to respond to an emergency involving a commercial nuclear power plant. An exercise is an event that tests the integrated capability and a major portion of the basic elements existing within emergency preparedness plans and organizations.

These exercises are conducted in accordance with FEMA regulations, which appear in 44 CFR part 350. Section 350.5(a) specifies that NUREG-0654/FEMA-REP-1 is to be used in reviewing and evaluating State and local government radiological emergency plans and preparedness.

FEMA's Exercise Evaluation Guidance

FEMA's Radiological Emergency Preparedness Exercise Manual (REP-14, dated 9/91) established 34 objectives that interpreted and applied the guidance contained in NUREG-0654.

In April 2002, FEMA revised REP-14 to present a new methodology for evaluating exercises. An interim program manual presenting the new methodology was issued in August 2002. That methodology adopts a new overall philosophy of evaluation and organizes the exercise evaluation into six broad areas.

Evaluation Philosophy

The objective of an emergency response plan is to protect the health and safety of the public and emergency responders. The goal of an exercise is to determine how well the implemented plan achieves that objective.

Exercise evaluation focuses on the big picture–the results: Did the organization accomplish what was intended? Were the health and safety of the public and emergency responders protected?

Looking at the Big Picture

Imagine looking at an impressionistic painting up close. At very close range, you can't identify what's in the painting. But if you step back and look at the painting as a whole, the image comes into better focus. The same is true with exercise evaluation: if you step back and look at the big picture, you'll have a better idea of whether the mission was accomplished.

The Plan Is the Basis

The emergency plan provides a framework to enable local officials to protect the health and safety of the public. Its main purpose is to assemble sufficient expertise, resources, and officials to address the emergency situation.

In an exercise, the plan and procedures are expected to be followed. That is, response activities should be based on emergency plans and procedures and completed as they actually would be in an emergency, unless otherwise indicated in the Extent of Play.

However, not everything in a plan may be applicable for a given scenario. Responders should not be so tied to a plan that they cannot take actions that would better protect the public. In cases like these, the evaluation looks at overall results rather than strict adherence to the plan.

Streamlined Process

This streamlined, outcome-oriented evaluation philosophy is embodied in the form now used to document exercise evaluation.

Evaluators now use a simplified document called the Evaluation Module to evaluate each criterion. This form contains only one question: Was this criterion adequately demonstrated?

Summary

To summarize the evaluation philosophy:

- Response actions are to be based on the emergency plan and procedures.
- The evaluation focuses on results: Are the health and safety of the public and the responders protected? Did any negative effects or potential effects result from responders' actions or lack of action?

- Responders have some latitude to use their judgment and depart from the plan when appropriate—as long as the objectives are met and the mission is accomplished.
- Evaluators focus on whether the criterion was adequately demonstrated.

Evaluation Methodology

The revision to REP-14 ushered in a new evaluation methodology. In this methodology, exercises are evaluated in six functional areas:

1. Emergency Operations Management—Evaluates the capability to alert, notify, and mobilize emergency personnel and to activate and staff emergency facilities.
2. Protective Action Decisionmaking—Assesses the ability to render decisions about what protective actions members of the public and emergency workers need to take in the wake of an incident.
3. Protective Action Implementation—Assesses the ability to implement protective actions, including evacuation.
4. Field Measurement and Analysis—Assesses the capability to conduct and analyze field radiation measurements, including plume phase and post-plume phase measurements and laboratory operations.
5. Emergency Notification and Public Information—Looks at the ability to notify the public of an incident and to effectively communicate protective action decisions.
6. Support Operations/Facilities—Assesses the capability to account for, monitor, and decontaminate evacuees, emergency workers, and emergency worker equipment; to provide temporary care of evacuees; and to ensure that capabilities exist for transporting and treating injured individuals who have been exposed to radiation.

Sub-Elements and Criteria

For organizational purposes, each evaluation area is divided into sub-elements. Each sub-element includes one or more criteria, which are the crux of the evaluation. Evaluators are assigned specific criteria to evaluate.

The Evaluation Module

Evaluations are documented on a form called the Evaluation Module. There is one Evaluation Module for each criterion. The Evaluation Module provides the following information to guide the evaluator during the exercise:

- Evaluation Area number and title
- Sub-element number and title
- Criterion number, description, and NUREG-0654 references
- Sub-element intent
- Extent of Play (generic and, if applicable, exercise-specific)

After the exercise, the evaluator records the following information on the Evaluation Module:

- Identifying information (name, site, etc.)
- Response to the question: Was this Criterion adequately demonstrated?
- Narrative of what transpired during the exercise, including prior issues.
- Identification and discussion of potential issues, including condition, possible cause, cross-references (to NUREG-0654, regulation, etc.), effect, and recommendation.

Extent of Play

Each criterion is described by an Extent of Play, which:

- Identifies demonstrations and simulations.
- Indicates what evaluators should look for.
- Specifies acceptable simulation limits.

An Extent of Play is provided with the Evaluation Module, for general reference only. Before the exercise, the Regional Assistance Committee (RAC) chair and the OROs agree upon what the exercise will accomplish, the criteria to be evaluated, and the Extent of Play for each criterion.

Overview: The Role of the Evaluator

Exercise evaluators are the eyes and ears of FEMA. The role of the evaluator is to observe, evaluate, and document what occurs in the assigned area during the exercise. Exercise documentation is important at several levels:

- Evaluation modules are used by the FEMA region to prepare the overall exercise report.
- Exercise reports are provided to the NRC as documentation of exercise findings and remedial actions.
- Exercise reports may be used by FEMA and NRC witnesses during any hearings before the Atomic Safety and Licensing Board.

As an evaluator, your role is key to a successful exercise evaluation.

Phases of Evaluation

The job of an exercise evaluator can be divided into three main phases: before the exercise, during the exercise, and after the exercise.

- Before the exercise: Evaluators prepare for the assignment by researching relevant portions of the jurisdiction's plan, the assigned evaluation criteria, and the Extent of Play.
- During the exercise: Evaluators observe, evaluate, and document response activities. While observing, they must remain objective and as unobtrusive as possible to avoid interfering in the exercise process.
- After the exercise: Evaluators prepare evaluation modules documenting what they have observed. These documents are used in compiling an overall report of the exercise.

Evaluator Job Skills

The main skills you need during the three phases include:

Pre-Exercise	Exercise	Post-Exercise
Reviewing Learning	Observing Documenting Recording	Evaluating Writing
Meeting Preparing	Interviewing	Reporting

To be effective you must apply the needed skills at the appropriate time. Notice that being an evaluator does NOT require you to be a policy expert or to be a decisionmaker about issues arising during the exercise.

The Evaluation Team

As an evaluator, you will not be alone. Each evaluator is assigned to a team, and every team has a team leader. The teams together make up the overall evaluation team, which encompasses all of the exercise locations.

You will be assigned an evaluation area and specific criteria to review. Chances are, others will be looking at some of the same criteria as you, and you may need to coordinate your data gathering and evaluation with them.

Assignments are normally made at least 45 days before the exercise and are based on each evaluator's ability. Newer evaluators are usually given less complex roles, while more experienced evaluators usually serve as team leaders or are assigned the more difficult criteria. Team leaders guide their team members in producing an effective evaluation and review their evaluation modules. Everyone assigned is needed. If you are unable to fulfill your assignment, you must promptly notify the appropriate individual so that a replacement can be found.

Exercise Evaluation Activities

An exercise might take place on only one day, but as an evaluator you may need to be on site for up to a week. When you arrive at the site, you will attend a series of meetings to coordinate the exercise activities and complete preparations for carrying out your assignment. After the exercise, there will be debriefings, report writing, and a public meeting.

Lesson 3: Evaluator Responsibilities

LESSON OVERVIEW

This lesson describes the evaluator's responsibilities before, during, and after an exercise.

Lesson Objectives

At the completion of this lesson, you will be able to:

- Identify the key responsibilities of the evaluator.
- Explain when it is appropriate to correct issues immediately.
- List and describe the steps included in a preliminary feedback session.
- Describe the documentation and reporting requirements for REP exercises.

BEFORE THE EXERCISE

The Evaluator Packet

When you are given an evaluator assignment, you will receive an evaluator packet containing some very important materials:

- Your assignment.
- Instructions.
- A Pre-Exercise Evaluator Preparation Guide for your assigned evaluation criteria.
- Jurisdiction information such as the response plan, procedures, Extent of Play, and prior issues.

These materials will form the basis of your preparation, and thorough preparation is critical for effective evaluation.

What Does Preparation Involve?

Evaluation begins with research. Preparing for your assignment involves:

- Becoming familiar with the jurisdiction.
- Correlating criteria with the plan and procedures.
- Analyzing the scenario, timelines, and Extent of Play.
- Creating a list of actions.
- Developing a data collection plan.
- Attending pre-exercise meetings.

Becoming Familiar with the Jurisdiction

Various types of communities may be involved in the exercise, including:

- Towns
- Cities
- Parishes
- Federal, public, and tribal lands
- States
- Counties

All of these jurisdictions can be involved in offsite emergency response. Carefully study the response plan to understand your jurisdiction's part in the overall response effort.

Jurisdiction Characteristics and Differences

Communities will have some things in common in their emergency response approach. For example, each plan must have certain emergency response functions, as outlined in the NUREG-0654/FEMA-REP-1 planning standards. However, the communities may differ in other aspects, including their:

- Organizational structure.
- History.
- Environment.
- Geopolitical boundaries.

You need to become familiar with the involved communities and be sensitive to any cultural differences that exist. Again—read the plan and ask questions if needed.

Jurisdiction Organizational Structure

States differ in the organizational structures they use for emergency management. In some States, the local governments are the major decisionmakers, with the State government providing support. In other States, the structure is just the opposite.

Researching the plan and other jurisdiction documents provided in the evaluator packet will help you understand the organizational structure for emergency management.

Correlating Criteria With the Plan

An important part of preparing for your assignment is studying the response plan and the implementing procedures to determine where each criterion is addressed and what is required. For example, let's say your area of responsibility includes:

Criterion 3.d.1: Appropriate traffic and access control is established.

Accurate instructions are provided to traffic and access control personnel.

You would need to review the plan and procedures to find the provisions that relate to this criterion. Examples of the types of preparatory questions you might ask include:

- Who is responsible for establishing traffic and/or access control points (TCP/ACPs)?
- Are pre-identified TCP/ACPs established in the plan?
- Is there coordination among various Offsite Response Organizers (OROs), such as local and State law enforcement, National Guard, and State and local transportation departments?
- When would TCP/ACPs be established?
- Who deploys TCP/ACP personnel to the assigned location?
- What agency is contacted for control of water, rail, and air traffic? Who notifies them, and when?

The REP Exercise Preparation Guide in your packet will help you ask the right questions to prepare to evaluate each criterion. The questions in the Prep Guide are for preparation, not to be used during the exercise!

Analyzing the Extent of Play

In preparation for the exercise, you must know the specific Extent of Play for each criterion you are evaluating. Studying the Extent of Play and related materials (e.g., scenario, timelines, prior issues) will help you understand:

- How the scenario will unfold (when events will occur)
- What activities will be demonstrated or simulated
- What demonstrations will occur out of sequence
- What to look for as indicators of adequate performance
- What prior issues are to be evaluated

Based on this information, you should develop a list of actions expected at your location for your assignment.

Developing a Data Collection Plan

Next, think about how you will collect the required information to determine if criteria are adequately demonstrated. Developing a data collection plan is important because the Evaluation Module does not include "prompts" in the way of questions. You must plan your own benchmarks for evaluating the criteria. Your data collection plan may include:

- Observation points (events and indicators to look for).

- Interviews to be conducted.
- Specific information to be obtained through interview or observation.
- Player-produced materials (e.g., logs, sign-in rosters, announcements, messages) to be collected.
- Information to be coordinated with other evaluators.

Based on this information, you should develop a list of actions expected at your location for your assignment.

In planning for data collection, consider the following factors:

- What is the end result we are looking for?
- What information is needed?
- Who else on the team is evaluating the same criteria?
- Will you need to collect data and materials from other evaluators?
- What does the team leader expect?

Pre-Exercise Meetings

Before the exercise, you will attend one or more preparation meetings, such as a pre-exercise briefing and team meetings. These meetings are your opportunity to learn more about the exercise and raise any questions you may have.

Ground Rules. One of the topics that will be discussed at the pre-exercise briefing are ground rules for the exercise–how the evaluation is expected to be carried out. Ground rules discussions usually address such questions as:

- What is my role during the exercise?
- How do I find out information that is not obvious, like who a player was talking to on the phone and what was discussed?
- If a reporter from the local newspaper or television station tries to interview me, or asks for information about the exercise, what should I do?
- What should I do if a real emergency occurs during the exercise?
- When and how are pre-exercise site visits to be conducted?
- How are meals handled during an exercise?

Your Questions. During your research and planning, be sure to identify any questions you need to have clarified during the pre-exercise meetings.

A Checklist

You should receive the following items, either in the evaluator packet or at the pre-exercise meetings. If you don't, be sure to ask!

- Assignment and preparation materials.

- Scenario information (description, ECLs).
- Policy on immediate correction of potential issues, preliminary direct feedback, and narratives and issues.
- Evaluation logistics (e.g., method of reporting time, arrival time, contact numbers, who gathers player documents, deadlines for work products).
- Previous Area Requiring Corrective Action (ARCA) forms.
- Answers to any questions you have about the exercise, Extent of Play requirements, and demonstration issues.

DURING THE EXERCISE

Getting Started

How you get started in your role as an evaluator affects how effective you will be. Suggestions for getting started include:

- o Get started right.
    - Arrive 15 to 30 minutes before any scheduled activity.
    - Bring appropriate clothing for the season and assignment. For most exercise locations, this means business attire.
    - Wear identification. Security may not let you in without it.
- Establish a rapport with the controller and players. Introduce yourself to the controller and key participants. Remember, exercise players will be aware that you are evaluating them. They may be nervous and apprehensive because they want to do a good job. So try to put them at ease and establish good rapport from the outset. The controller will manage exercise activities. Establishing a rapport with this person will your job run smoothly.
- Arrange for copies. Be sure arrangements have been made to receive copies of all logs, messages (including EAS messages), sign-in rosters, notification forms, and other materials developed during the exercise. Don't leave your location without these, unless instructed otherwise by the RAC Chair Team Leader or Site Specialist.

Observing the Action

One of your most important tasks is observing the action. You are the eyes and ears of FEMA. You will play a key role in determining whether what you see and hear meets the performance requirements in your evaluation area.

While focusing on your assigned criteria, you should also observe and record as much of the pertinent activity outside your primary area of responsibility as possible.

Guidelines for conducting your observations include the following:

Be Objective. Objectivity is at the heart of evaluation. Be sure to:

- Watch, listen, and take notes.
- Document what you see and hear and what should have occurred but did not.
- Be certain of the facts you record.
- Don't mix fact with opinion.
- Develop a detailed time record for observed events.

The guide for your observations, and the basis for documenting those observations, is the Evaluation Module form. After the exercise, you will complete one Evaluation Module for each criterion assigned to you.

Be Alert. Stay "tuned in" and pay attention:

- Look at the log and wait for the event you are trying to observe.
- Be available and ready to observe at the correct time.
- Move around–be in the right place at the right time.
    o Don't let mealtimes interfere with your evaluation.
    o Minimize "Evaluator Impact." Remember, you're an observer, not a participant.
- Don't give instructions or orders during the exercise.
- Don't help players decide what to do.
- Don't interpret the plan or procedures for them.
- Never reveal the scenario to the players.

And remember, evaluators have no authority to terminate the exercise.

Remain as Unobtrusive as Possible. In a nutshell–stay out of the way! Don't interfere with exercise play, and don't be a distraction. For example:

- Avoid using ORO communications equipment that could interfere with the players.
- If you have questions about exercise play, ask the exercise Controller or other designated contact person.
- Refer questions from media to the designated contact.

But do ask questions as needed to complete your evaluation. We'll discuss interviewing techniques next.

Interviewing Players

At times you may need to interview players to complete your evaluation. This may occur for a variety of reasons, such as:

- There are many activities to observe, and you cannot be in all places at once.
- You need to confirm that an action did or did not take place.
- Players did not document an action. Asking questions is especially critical for simulation or walk-through interviews.

Effective Interviewing

To ensure that your interviews accomplish what you intend, remember two things:

- Interviews should always have a clear purpose. Remember, the purpose is to get information, not to try to stump the players!
    - Interviews require planning. Determine beforehand the best way to get the information you need. (If possible, make this part of your data collection plan.) If you can directly observe something, there is probably no reason to ask extensive questions.
    - For maximum interview effectiveness, apply the 4 T's:
- Terminology: Avoid confusion by using the language and terms that are used in the players' plans and procedures.
- Tone: Use an appropriate tone: don't be adversarial or accusatory. You are merely seeking information.
- Timing: Ask questions at appropriate times–during down times, after the actions you're asking about are complete. This avoids interrupting players or prompting them to take actions they may have forgotten.
- Techniques: Learn and use effective questioning and listening techniques to get the most out of interviews.

Asking Questions

One method for keeping an interview on track is to use different types of questions depending on the type of information needed. The five types of questions (open, closed, hypothetical, probing, and leading) have slightly different applications, as shown in the following table.

Interview Questions

Question Type	Description/Uses	Examples
Open Question	• Encourages the flow of information. • Requires more complex answers than just "yes" or "no." • Often begins with who, what, when, where, why, or how.	• What happens when the ALERT ECL comes in? • How would the TCP be set up? • What factors do you consider when authorizing excess exposure?
Closed Question	• Controls the flow of information. • Is direct and focused. • Calls for straight and simple answers.	• What time was the facility activated? • What notifications have been made?
Hypothetical Question	• Poses a "What if" scenario. • Not designed to stump the	• What would you do if there was a traffic accident on the major evacuation route? • What would you

	players. • Useful in walk-throughs and simulations.	do if a person showed up at the CCC and did not have evidence of being monitored for contamination?
Probing Question	• Used for followup, to draw out additional information. • Aims for depth rather than breadth.	[Following the answer to an open question] • Can you give me some examples of situations where that might occur? • What would you do next?
Leading Question	• May indicate a preferred answer. • No place in REP evaluations.	• Your plan says you have 25 dosimeters—is that right? • I would call the schools now, wouldn't you? • The order came in to issue KI a few minutes ago. Have you issued the KI yet?

Effective Listening

The success of your interview will depend to a great extent on your ability to accurately hear and process the responses.

Effective listening can be broken down into four key elements:

- Hear the message—LISTEN.
- Interpret the message—CONFIRM.
- Evaluate the message—PROBE.
- Respond to the message—UNDERSTAND.

Confirming is an important step in ensuring that you understand the message. A useful approach is to mentally summarize the themes being discussed and periodically restate in your words the main points. Don't parrot back the exact words you heard!

Paraphrasing helps ensure that you heard the person correctly and understood what they meant to say. Paraphrasing often begins with such phrases as:

- "If I understood you correctly . . ."
- "So you're saying . . .,"
- "You're concerned because . . .,"
- "In other words . . .."

Taking Notes

As you conduct your observations and interviews, it is very important to take notes. Don't trust your memory! Your notes will form the basis for analyzing what you have seen and heard. Following these guidelines will make your note-taking more effective:

- Be brief. Develop your own shorthand and record important facts or key words. Don't fill out the Evaluation Module or write summaries during the action. Brevity is especially important during interviews; taking lengthy notes while someone is talking will not convey your interest!
- Be objective. Don't mix facts with opinions.
- Write clearly. Write clearly and legibly to use notes later in preparing the evaluation module.
- Be thorough. In addition to recording what you see and hear, record information that is posted on displays.
- Keep a log. Keep a personal log of exercise activities–especially significant events.

Correcting Issues Immediately

In very limited instances, you may have exercise participants re-demonstrate an activity found to have been unsatisfactorily performed. Whether immediate correction will be permitted, and what activities will be eligible for re-demonstration, are negotiated before the exercise as part of the Extent of Play.

Key points to remember about immediate correction include:

- Immediate correction is used primarily during tabletop exercises, drills, and out-ofsequence demonstrations.
- In an integrated exercise, the re-demonstration cannot interfere with the exercise or affect other evaluation areas.
- Agreement is reached during Extent of Play negotiations on whether re-demonstration is permitted and which activities are eligible. Find out what is allowed before the exercise!
- The ORO may give on-the-spot refresher training before the re-demonstration.
- The RAC chair makes the determination about how to classify the issues, based on the evaluator's documentation.

Documenting the Action

Following the exercise, you will prepare a complete and detailed written summary of potential issues, which may include planning issues and performance issues. The RAC chairperson/Region will use this report in compiling an overall report of the exercise.

Actual preparation of your exercise report will happen after the exercise. However, during the exercise you will need to document your observations in enough detail to allow you to generate an effective report later. The Evaluation Module form provides the framework for documenting the action.

During the exercise you should make note of:

- Actions observed: Who (title, not name), what, where, when, how.
- Whether the criterion was adequately demonstrated.
- Deviations from the plan or procedures, even if you did not directly observe a negative impact.
- Actions and lack of action that you believe are potential issues (we'll talk more about issues in a moment).
- Demonstrations not in accordance with the Extent of Play. (However, you should work with the Controller to ensure that demonstrations are in accordance with the Extent of Play.)
- Unsatisfactorily demonstrated actions that were immediately corrected.

Documenting Potential Issues

A plan issue is defined as an observed or identified inadequacy in the ORO's emergency plan or implementing procedures, rather than in the ORO's performance. Plan issues may be identified by the evaluator or reviewer, but are classified as such by the RAC Chairperson. However, plan issues are not considered to be exercise issues and will not necessarily be included in the exercise report. Plan issues may be provided to the State(s) for correction via letter from the Regional Director within 90 days of the exercise.

For example, the phone number is incorrect in the plan/procedure. But the staff member is contacted successfully by another means. The plan needs to be fixed to correct phone number or to use the other means which was successful.

An exercise issue is a problem in organizational performance that is linked with specific NUREG-0654 standards and applicable evaluation criteria. (The applicable standards and criteria are cited in the evaluation area criteria.) There are two categories of exercise issues:

- Deficiencies, and
- Areas requiring corrective action (ARCAs).

Exercise evaluators only identify potential issues. Classification of issues is made by the RAC Chair (sometimes in consultation with FEMA HQ) after feedback has been received from all evaluators and participants.

Issue Elements

When documenting potential issues, five issue elements must be included:

- Condition: Description of the inadequacy.
- Possible cause: What is responsible.
- Reference: Cross-references to the plan, procedures, NUREG-0654, and/or Extent of Play.
- Effect: What resulted, or could have resulted, from this issue.

- Recommendation: How to correct the problem.

The notes you take during the exercise should enable you to complete this documentation after the exercise.

Analyzing Your Observations

Analysis is a very important part of your job. You are not simply making note of what you see. As an evaluator, you must analyze, assess, and evaluate what you observe. For example:

- What actions or inaction will you identify as potential issues?
- What was the effect—or potential effect—of the actions or inaction?
- What details can you cite to support the identification of potential issues?

Your analysis of ORO performance will continue after the exercise, as you coordinate with other evaluators and develop your report.

Giving Preliminary Direct Feedback

Right after the exercise is a good time to give feedback on strengths and weaknesses you observed. This feedback is preliminary, for several reasons:

- Evaluators do not make a final determination whether a concern is an exercise issue (this is the RAC chair's job).
- The evaluators have not had time at this point to analyze their notes and the player documents.
- Each evaluator has seen only one part of the exercise.

Your team may wish to meet, as soon as the exercise ends, to develop initial positive and negative observations. When you have reached agreement, you can conduct a brief feedback session among the evaluators and participants at your location.

Strategies for effective preliminary direct feedback include:

- Schedule in advance. Establish the time, place, and audience for the feedback session before the exercise begins.
- Set the stage. Characterize your comments as preliminary observations.
- Balance positive and negative. Acknowledge everyone's participation and mention the strengths and high points of their performance. Describe problems that you saw and recommend improvements based on your experience.
- Be brief. Keep feedback short and to the point, without lengthy discussion. Confine your feedback to the criteria you evaluated.
- Be direct. Be tactfully direct, without sugarcoating. Refer to people by titles, not names.

- Choose terms carefully. Avoid such terms as "Deficiency," "ARCA," and "Planning Issue." The RAC chair will classify exercise issues after receiving feedback from all evaluators and participants.
- Seek input. This is your last opportunity to obtain information from the participants. Solicit their input and listen to their perspective.
- Inform. Announce future post-exercise meetings.

AFTER THE EXERCISE

Key tasks to be completed after the exercise include:

- Coordinating with other evaluators.
- Giving preliminary direct feedback.
- Participating in post-exercise meetings.
- Developing your Evaluation Modules.

Comprehensive Analysis

In evaluating an exercise, we look at functions in two ways: horizontally and vertically.

- Was the function adequately demonstrated horizontally (e.g., communication inside your location, Emergency Operations Centers (EOCs))?
- Was the function adequately demonstrated vertically throughout the entire response organization (e.g., communication between the EOC and local response organizations)?

This comprehensive analysis is required to determine if there was an effect, or a potential effect, of an exercise participant's action.

Coordinating With Other Evaluators

As you gather, assess, and analyze information, you may find a need to coordinate with other evaluators at your location or at another location to get the full picture of what occurred. Coordinating with other evaluators enables you to fill in the missing pieces of the evaluation puzzle.

For example, an evaluator at an EOC needs to coordinate with the evaluator at the EAS radio station to determine times of key events such as simulated EAS message broadcasts.

Participating in Post-Exercise Meetings

The initial team meeting after the exercise is only the first of what may be several debriefing meetings you will take part in. At these meetings, you will have an opportunity to:

- Provide input to the exercise timeline. (One of the tasks completed in the postexercise debriefing is to piece together the various evaluators' event logs into one consolidated timeline. When evaluators' logs differ, judgments must be made about the most reasonable timeline.)
- Discuss any problems you identified with the exercise play at your location.
- Discuss your evaluation with the other evaluators to develop the complete picture of the play.
- Prepare narratives and complete your evaluation modules.

Completing Your Evaluation Modules

Documentation of your evaluation begins during the exercise and continues in the completion of your Evaluation Module(s). You will complete one Evaluation Module for each criterion within your assignment or contribute to another team member's module. There are three parts to the Evaluation Module:

- A question.
- The narrative.
- An issues section.

Question. Only one question needs to be answered: Was this criterion adequately demonstrated? The question has three possible answers:

YES: The desired result was achieved—whether or not it was done in accordance with the plans/procedures. If it was not done in accordance with the plans/procedures, then a planning issue (not an exercise performance issue) would likely be identified.

NO: The desired result was not achieved. This might be due to the Extent of Play not being followed.

N/A: Designates an activity or function that does not require demonstration under the emergency plans or that is specified as not required in the Extent of Play agreement.

Narrative. Each criterion requires a written narrative of what transpired. Be sure each narrative you write:

- Is a logical discussion of events.
- Supports your recommendation that the criterion was or was not adequately demonstrated.

  - o Contains the following information:
    - All the vital information
    - Effect
    - Supporting detail
    - Previous ARCA demonstrations
    - Any items that were immediately corrected

Narrative Content

- Vital information includes who, what, where, when, why, and how–as applicable to the specific criterion you are evaluating. You must use your knowledge of the evaluation criterion, your detailed notes, player documents, and the Extent of Play to guide you.
- Effect is an important part of the narrative. If there is an observed weakness, the narrative must address the effect on the ORO's ability to accomplish assigned tasks.
  - o Supporting detail must be provided for any issues identified. Regions differ on the amount of detail required, so check with your team leader/RAC chair.
  - o But be careful—don't draw conclusions without supporting facts. For example, state "No evidence of annual calibration," not "Instruments were not calibrated."
- Previous ARCA demonstrations, if any, require discussion, including whether they have been resolved, the corrective action demonstrated, and a detailed discussion of the actions accomplished to resolve the ARCA. If the ARCA has not been resolved, identify it as an "Unresolved ARCA" and describe in detail the reason for this conclusion.
  - o Immediate corrections should be discussed, including:
    - The initial unsatisfactory performance.
    - Any refresher training given.
    - Whether the re-demonstration was adequate.

Evaluation Module: Issues

As part of your evaluation, you should document any actions or lack of action that you believe are potential issues. This includes any deviations from the plan or procedures–even if you did not directly observe a negative impact. You may need to confer with other evaluators to determine whether there was an impact.

Performance issues will be included in the final exercise report—but, remember, your potential issues may or may not make it into the final exercise report. The RAC chair responsible for developing the report will consider your issues in the context of the entire exercise.

Planning issues will be put in a separate letter to the ORO.

Issue Elements

Each Evaluation Module has a page for identifying potential issues. This is where you will write up the five issue elements mentioned earlier:

- Condition—Description of the inadequacy.
- Possible cause—What created the issue; responsibility.
- Reference—Cross-reference to the plan, procedures, NUREG-0654, and/or the Extent of Play. Some regions require the evaluator to look up the specific NUREG0654 element; consult your team leader.
- Effect—Discussion of what resulted, or could have resulted, from this issue.
- Recommendation—Suggestions on how to correct the issue.

Lesson 4: EA-1—Emergency Operations Management

LESSON OVERVIEW

This lesson provides information on Evaluation Area 1, Emergency Operations

Management.

Lesson Objectives

At the completion of this lesson, you will be able to:

- Identify the five elements to be evaluated under emergency operations management.
- Summarize the criteria used to evaluate emergency operations management.

OVERVIEW OF EVALUATION AREA 1

EA-1, Emergency Operations Management, is divided into 5 sub-elements:

1.a Mobilization

1.b Facilities

1.c Direction and Control

1.dCommunications Equipment

1.e Equipment and Supplies to Support Operations

Each sub-element is evaluated in every exercise. All activities must be based on the ORO's plans and procedures and completed as they would be in an actual emergency unless otherwise indicated in the Extent of Play agreement.

1.a: MOBILIZATION

Sub-element 1.a, Mobilization, deals with the capability to alert, notify, and mobilize emergency personnel and activate facilities in a timely manner. Mobilization includes one criterion: 1.a.1: OROs use effective procedures to alert, notify, and mobilize emergency personnel and activate facilities in a timely manner.

What the Policy Requires

During the exercise, OROs should demonstrate the capability to:

- Receive notification of an emergency situation from the licensee.
- Verify the notification.
- Contact, alert, and mobilize key emergency personnel in a timely manner. (Timely manner means "with a sense of urgency and without undue (excessive) delay.")
- Activate facilities for immediate use by mobilized personnel.

Staff may be pre-positioned at facilities beyond a normal commuting distance and for out-of-sequence demonstrations.

Reviewing Plans and Procedures

Mobilization activities must be based on the ORO's plans and procedures. In preparing

for evaluation, you should review the plans and procedures to determine:

- How the ORO is notified of the emergency classification level (ECL), and by whom.
- What happens when the ECL changes (e.g., notifications; changes in staffing).
- Whether verification of ECL changes is required.
- What the key positions within the EOC/facility are, and which ones require 24-hour staffing.
- What the criteria are for declaring the EOC activated and operational.

Reviewing the Extent of Play

Mobilization activities must be completed as they would be in an actual emergency unless otherwise indicated in the Extent of Play agreement. In preparing for evaluation, you should review the Extent of Play agreement to determine how it impacts this criterion. For example:

- Does it allow for pre-positioning of any participants?
- Does it allow for any simulation?
- Are any out-of-sequence demonstrations required? If so, what, when, and where?

Evaluating the Criterion

In evaluating this criterion:

- Look for activities performed according to the plan/procedures and the Extent of Play agreement.
- Note any pre-positioning of staff (is it consistent with the Extent of Play agreement?).
- Record the times of all key events.
- Obtain copies of the sign-in log, notifications received, and player logs.

1.b: FACILITIES

Sub-element 1.b, Facilities, consists of one criterion: 1.b.1: Facilities are sufficient

to support the emergency response.

Facilities are evaluated for this criterion, as a baseline, during the first exercise under the new Evaluation Criteria. Thereafter, they are evaluated only if they are new or have substantial changes in structure or mission. The Extent of Play should indicate if this is the case.

What the Policy Requires

Responsible OROs should demonstrate the availability of facilities that support the

accomplishment of emergency operations. Areas to be considered include:

- Adequate space
- Furnishings
- Lighting
- Restrooms
- Ventilation
- Backup power and/or alternate facility (if required to support operations)

Reviewing Plans, Procedures, and Extent of Play

In preparing for evaluation, you should review the plans, procedures, and Extent of

Play agreement to determine:

- What should be available in the way of space, furnishings, lighting, restrooms, ventilation, and backup power or alternate facilities to support emergency operations conducted from the facility?

- Do the plan or procedures include a diagram or floor plan of the facility?

Evaluating the Criterion

Items to check during the exercise include:

- Is the facility set up as shown on the floor plan?
- Is it operated according to the ORO's plan/procedure unless otherwise indicated in the Extent of Play?
- If not, did it cause any adverse consequences?
- Are changes to the plan or procedures recommended as a result?

1.c DIRECTION AND CONTROL

Sub-element 1.c, Direction and Control, deals with the OROs' ability to control their

overall response to an emergency. Direction and Control includes one criterion:

1.c.1: Key personnel with leadership roles for the ORO provide direction and control to that part of the overall response effort for which they are responsible.

Direction and control issues tend to have a ripple effect, creating an impact on other criteria. Vertical evaluation would involve looking at direction and control as a whole in the exercise, throughout all locations where it was evaluated.

What the Policy Says

Leadership personnel should demonstrate the ability to carry out essential functions of

the response effort, such as:

- Keeping the staff informed (e.g., through periodic briefings).
- Coordinating with other appropriate OROs.
- Ensuring completion of requirements and requests.

There may be more than one "leader" at your site. For example, in an EOC the Emergency Management Director is usually in charge, but there might be others (e.g., an Operations Section Chief).

Direction and control activities must be performed based on the ORO's plans and procedures as they would in an actual emergency unless otherwise indicated in the Extent of Play agreement.

1.d COMMUNICATIONS EQUIPMENT

Sub-element 1.d, Communications Equipment, relates to the establishment of reliable primary and backup communication systems to ensure communications with key emergency personnel. This includes personnel at such organizations as:

- Appropriate contiguous governments within the EPZ.
- Federal emergency response organizations.
- The licensee and its facilities.
- Emergency Operations Centers (EOCs).
- Field teams.

The Communications Equipment sub-element has one criterion: 1.d.1: At least two communication systems are available, at least one operates properly, and communication links are established and maintained with appropriate locations. Communications capabilities are managed in support of emergency operations.

What the Policy Requires

The ORO must demonstrate capability in these key areas:

- Full functionality of a primary and at least one backup system.
- Use of communications equipment and procedures, as needed, for transmission and receipt of exercise messages between facilities and field units.
- Access by all facilities and field teams to at least one communication system that is independent of the commercial telephone system and uses a separate power source.
- System management that ensures timely handling of messages.
- Coordinated communication link for fixed and mobile medical support facilities.

Use of Backup Systems

During exercises we expect primary systems to be used and to work properly. If they do not, backups will be used. The ORO must demonstrate the primary system and at least one backup.

- If one system fails but there is no adverse effect or potential effect, no performance issue is assigned.
- If both systems fail, there is no issue if additional backups are used, work properly, and there is no adverse effect.

In all cases, communications systems that fail must be fixed no later than the next

scheduled communications drill.

1.e EQUIPMENT AND SUPPLIES TO SUPPORT OPERATIONS

Sub-element 1.e, Equipment and Supplies to Support Operations, deals with the ORO having emergency equipment and supplies adequate to support the emergency response. This sub-element has one criterion: 1.e.1: Equipment, maps, displays, dosimetry, potassium iodide (KI), and other supplies are sufficient to support emergency operations.

Equipment and Supplies Requirements

Equipment and supplies within the facility should be sufficient and consistent with the facility's assigned emergency operations role. Key provisions relate to:

- Use of maps and displays.
- Inspection, inventory, operational checking, and calibration of instruments.
- Availability of dosimetry and dosimeter chargers.
- Maintenance of potassium iodide (KI) inventories.
- Inspection of storage locations.
- Availability of traffic and access control equipment.

Lesson 5: EA-2 — Protective Action Decisionmaking

LESSON OVERVIEW

This lesson provides information on Evaluation Area 2, Protective Action Decisionmaking.

Lesson Objectives

At the completion of this lesson, you will be able to:

- Identify the five elements to be evaluated under protective action decisionmaking.
- Summarize the criteria used to evaluate protective action decisionmaking.

OVERVIEW OF EVALUATION AREA 2

EA-2, Protective Action Decisionmaking, includes 5 sub-elements:

2.a Emergency Worker Exposure Control

2.b Radiological Assessment and Protective Action Recommendations and Decisions for the Plume Phase of the Emergency

2.c Protective Action Decisions for the Protection of Special Populations

2.d Radiological Assessment and Decisionmaking for the Ingestion Exposure Pathway

2.e Radiological Assessment and Decisionmaking Concerning Relocation, Reentry, and Return

All activities must be based on the ORO's plans and procedures and completed as they would be in an actual emergency unless otherwise indicated in the Extent of Play.

Evaluation Frequency

The minimum frequency for evaluating criteria under these sub-elements is as follows:

Sub-Elements	Minimum Frequency
2.a Emergency Worker Exposure Control 2.b Plume Phase 2.c Protection of Special Populations	Every Exercise
2.d Ingestion Exposure Pathway 2.e Relocation, Reentry, and Return	Once in 6 years. The plume phase and the post-plume phase can be demonstrated separately.

2.a EMERGENCY WORKER EXPOSURE CONTROL

Sub-element 2.a, Emergency Worker Exposure Control, assesses the ORO's ability to render decisions about what protective actions emergency workers need to take in the wake of an incident. This sub-element includes one criterion:

2.a.1: OROs use a decisionmaking process, considering relevant factors and appropriate coordination, to ensure that an exposure control system, including the use of KI, is in place for emergency workers including provisions to authorize radiation exposure in excess of administrative limits or protective action guides.

Radiation Exposure Limits

Radiation exposure limits for emergency workers are the recommended accumulated dose limits or exposure rates that emergency workers may be permitted to incur during an emergency.

These limits include any pre-established administrative reporting limits (taking into consideration Total Effective Dose Equivalent or organ-specific limits) identified in the ORO's plans and procedures.

Required Decisionmaking

This criterion applies to any ORO authorized to send emergency workers into the plume exposure pathway EPZ. The ORO must demonstrate the ability to make decisions regarding:

- Authorization of exposure levels above the pre-authorized levels.
- Number of emergency workers who can receive those higher levels.

- Distribution and administration of potassium iodide (KI) as a protective measure, based on:
    - The ORO's plan and/or procedures, or
    - Projected thyroid dose compared with the established Protective Action Guides (PAGs) for KI administration.

2.b PLUME PHASE

Sub-Element 2.b is Radiological Assessment and Protective Action Recommendations and Decisions for the Plume Phase of the Emergency. It provides that OROs have the capability to use all available data to independently project integrated dose and compare the estimated dose savings with the protective action guides.

OROs can choose, from among a range of protective actions, those that are most appropriate for the situation. They base these choices on PAGs from their plan/procedures. Or, they can base them on the EPA Manual of PAGs and Protective Actions for Nuclear Incidents (EPA 400-R-92-001) and other criteria, such as:

- Plant conditions
- Licensee protective action recommendations (PARs)
- Coordination of protective action decisions (PADs) with other political jurisdictions (for example, other affected OROs)
    - Availability of appropriate in-place shelter, weather conditions, and situations that create higher than normal risk from evacuation.
    - This sub-element is broken into two criteria related to PARs and PADs:
- Criterion 2.b.1: Appropriate PARs are based on available information on plant conditions, field monitoring data, and licensee and ORO dose projections, as well as knowledge of onsite and offsite environmental conditions.
- Criterion 2.b.2: A decisionmaking process involving consideration of appropriate factors and necessary coordination is used to make PADs for the general public (including the recommendation for the use of KI, if ORO policy).

Criterion 2.b.1: PARs

Requirements for Criterion 2.b.1 relate to:

- Appropriate means of PAR development
- Validation of dose projections
- Prompt transmittal of PARs
- Handling of differences in dose projections
- Revision of dose projections

Development of PARs

During the initial stage of the emergency response, following notification of plant conditions that may warrant offsite protective actions, the ORO should demonstrate its ability to use appropriate means to develop PARs for decisionmakers. The means for developing PARs are described in the plan and/or procedures. The ORO should also consider:

- Available information and recommendations from the licensee.
- Field monitoring data, if available.

When the licensee provides release and meteorological data, the ORO also considers

these data.

Dose Projections

Validation. The ORO should demonstrate a reliable capability to independently validate dose projections. The types of calculations to be demonstrated depend on the data available and the need for assessments to support the PARs appropriate to the scenario. In all cases, calculation of projected dose should be demonstrated. Projected doses should be related to quantities and units of the PAG to which they will be compared.

Prompt transmittal. PARs should be promptly transmitted to decisionmakers in a prearranged format.

Handling of projection differences. The ORO should discuss with the licensee any differences greater than a factor of 10 between projected doses by the licensee. Discussions should address the input data and assumptions used, the use of different models, or other possible reasons for the differences. Resolution of differences should be incorporated into the PAR if timely and appropriate.

Refinement of projections. The ORO should demonstrate the capability to use any additional data to refine projected doses and exposure rates and revise the associated PARs.

Criterion 2.b.2: PADs

Criterion 2.b.2 requires that a decisionmaking process involving consideration of appropriate factors and necessary coordination be used to make PADs for the general public (including the recommendation for the use of KI, if ORO policy).

Requirements relate primarily to initial and subsequent PADs, decisions on KI, and coordination. Evaluators need to be aware of planned coordination, both within States and among multiple States. Check the plan carefully to see what is required.

Initial PADs. Initial PADs need to be made in a timely manner appropriate to the

situation, and they PADs should be based on:

- Notification from the licensee
- Assessment of plant status and releases
    - PARs from the utility and ORO staff
    - Subsequent PADs. The decisionmakers should be able to change protective actions as appropriate based on subsequent projections. For example, subsequent PADs would be generated when dose assessment personnel provide additional PARs based on such input as:
- Later dose projections
- Field monitoring data
- Information on plant conditions

KI Decisions

If (and only if) it is in the ORO's plan to use potassium iodide (KI) as a protective measure for the general public, the ORO should demonstrate its ability to make decisions on the distribution and administration of KI to supplement sheltering and evacuation. Those decisions should be based on:

- The ORO's plan and/or procedures, or
- Projected thyroid dose compared with the established PAG for KI administration.

The KI decisionmaking process should involve close coordination with appropriate assessment and decisionmaking staff.

Coordination

Finally, criterion 2.b.2 addresses coordination with regard to plume phase protective action decisions. If more than one ORO is involved in decisionmaking, OROs should:

- Communicate and coordinate PADs with affected OROs.
- Demonstrate the capability to communicate the contents of decisions to the affected jurisdictions.

2.c SPECIAL POPULATIONS

Sub-element 2.c, Protective Action Decisions for the Protection of Special Populations,

includes one criterion:

2.c.1: Protective action decisions are made, as appropriate, for special population groups.

Examples of special populations include:

- Correctional facilities
- Hospitals and nursing homes
- Schools and day care centers
- Mobility-impaired or transportation-dependent individuals

Protective Actions

Protective actions for special populations who could be affected by a radiological release usually include:

- Evacuation
- Sheltering-in-place
    - Use of KI if applicable
    - Evacuation is usually implemented in areas where doses are projected to exceed the lower end of the range of PAGs. The exception would be for situations where high risk is involved. In cases involving a high-risk environment or high-risk groups (e.g., the immobile or infirm), various factors should be considered in protective action decisionmaking. Examples include:
- Weather conditions
- Shelter availability
- Availability of transportation assets
- Risk of evacuation versus risk from the avoided dose
- Precautionary school evacuations

In situations where an institutionalized population cannot be evacuated, the administration of KI should be considered.

Schools

Schools receive special emphasis under this criterion.

Alert and notification. OROs should demonstrate the ability to alert and notify all school systems/districts of emergency conditions that could necessitate protective actions for students. Contacts with school systems/districts must be actual.

Prompt decisions. OROs and/or officials of school systems/districts should demonstrate the capability to make prompt decisions on protective actions for students.

Decisionmaking process. Officials should demonstrate that the decisionmaking process for protective actions considers (i.e., automatically accepts them or to gives them heavy weight):

- PARs made by ORO personnel.
- The ECL at which these recommendations are received.
- Preplanned strategies for protective actions for that ECL.
- The location of students at the time (for example, whether the students are still at home, en route to the school, or at the school).

The decisionmaking process also needs to take into account the availability of

resources.

2.d INGESTION EXPOSURE PATHWAY

Sub-element 2.d is Radiological Assessment and Decisionmaking for the Ingestion Exposure Pathway. During a nuclear power plant incident, a radioactive release may contaminate water supplies and agricultural products in the surrounding areas. This would likely occur during the plume phase and could impact the ingestion pathway for weeks or years. 2.d addresses the ability to assess radiological consequences for the ingestion exposure pathway, relate them to PAGs, and make PADs to mitigate exposure. This sub-element includes one criterion:

2.d.1: Radiological consequences for the ingestion pathway is assessed and appropriate protective action decisions are made based on the ORO's planning criteria.

This criterion is evaluated once every 6 years. The plume phase and the post-plume phase (ingestion, relocation, re-entry, and return) can be demonstrated separately.

Precautionary Actions

OROs are expected to take precautionary actions to protect food and water supplies, or to minimize exposure to potentially contaminated water and food, in accordance with their plans/procedures. Precautionary actions (e.g., placing milk animals on stored feed or using protected water supplies) are often initiated based on the facility's ECLs.

Consequence Assessment

The ORO should use its procedures (for example, development of a sampling plan) to assess the radiological consequences of a release on the food and water supplies. The assessment should include:

- Evaluation of the radiological analyses of representative samples of water, food, and other locally relevant food products from potentially impacted areas.
- Characterization of the releases from the facility.
- The extent of areas potentially impacted by the release.

Agricultural and watershed data within the 50-mile EPZ should be considered in the assessment.

Providing Recommendations

Comparison to PAGs. The radiological impacts should be compared to the ingestion PAGs in the ORO's plan/procedures, which may be based on specific dose commitment criteria or on FDA guidance.

Timely and appropriate. Recommendations provided to ORO decisionmakers should be timely and appropriate. As time permits, the ORO may also include a comparison of taking or not taking a given action on the resultant ingestion pathway dose commitments.

Protective Action Decisions

The ORO then makes decisions to minimize radiological impacts from the ingestion pathway. Those decisions should be:

- Timely
- Based on the assessments and other available information
- Communicated to (and, if possible, coordinated with) neighboring and local OROs.

OROs are expected to use Federal resources and other resources (e.g., compacts, nuclear insurers) if they are available. Evaluation of this criterion will take into consideration the level of Federal and other resources participating.

2.e RELOCATION, REENTRY, AND RETURN

Sub-element 2.e is Radiological Assessment and Decisionmaking Concerning Relocation, Reentry, and Return. Decisions about relocation, reentry, and return are essential for the protection of the public from the direct long-term exposure to deposited radioactive materials from a severe incident at a nuclear power plant. Sub-element 2.e contains one criterion:

2.e.1: Timely relocation, re-entry, and return decisions are made and coordinated as appropriate, based on assessments of the radiological conditions and criteria in the ORO's plan and/or procedures.

This criterion is demonstrated once in 6 years. The plume phase and the post-plume

phase can be demonstrated separately.

Relocation

Relocation is the removal or continued exclusion of people from contaminated areas to avoid chronic radiation exposure. OROs should demonstrate their ability to:

- Estimate integrated dose in contaminated areas.
- Compare these estimates with PAGs.
- Apply decision criteria for relocation of members of the public who have not been evacuated but where projected doses exceed relocation PAGs.
- Control access to evacuated and restricted areas.

Decisions should also be made for relocating evacuees who lived in areas that now have residual radiation levels in excess of the PAGs. The areas to be restricted should be determined based on factors such as:

- The mix of radionuclides in deposited materials
- Calculated exposure rates versus the PAGs
- Field samples of vegetation and soil analyses

Re-Entry

Re-entry refers to provisions for the return of the public after evacuation, when the radiation risk has been reduced to acceptable levels. Decisions should be made regarding:

- Location of control points.
- Policies regarding access.
- Exposure control for emergency workers and members of the public who need to re-enter temporarily to perform specific tasks or missions.

Re-Entry Control Procedures

Examples of control procedures include:

- Use of dosimetry by emergency workers.
- Questioning people about why, where, and how long they need to be in the area.
- Having radiation exposure rate maps available.
- Providing advice on areas to avoid.
  - Implementing controlled exit procedures, such as:
    - Monitoring of individuals, vehicles, and equipment.
    - Decision criteria regarding decontamination.
    - Proper disposition of emergency worker dosimetry.
    - Maintenance of emergency worker radiation exposure records.

Individual Re-entry

Responsible OROs should have a strategy for authorizing re-entry of individuals into the restricted zone, based on established decision criteria. Their strategy should allow for modifying those policies for specific purposes, such as:

- Security (e.g., police patrols)
- Essential services (e.g., fire protection and utilities)
- Other critical functions
- Property maintenance or retrieval of important possessions by members of the public.

Policies should be in place for providing dosimetry to anyone allowed to re-enter the restricted zone.

Coordination

Coordinated policies for access and exposure control should be developed among all agencies with roles to perform in the restricted zone.

The extent to which OROs need to develop policies on re-entry will be determined by scenario events.

Return

Decisions about return are to be based on:

- Environmental data.
  - Identifiable political boundaries or geophysical features which demarcate areas to which the public may return.
  - Other factors that should be considered in return decisions include:
- Cancellation of the ECL and the relaxation of associated restrictive measures.
- Measurements of radiation from ground deposition.
- Services and facilities requiring restoration within a few days (e.g., medical and social services, utilities, roads, schools, and intermediate term housing for relocated persons).

Lesson 6: EA-3 — Protective Action Implementation

LESSON OVERVIEW

This lesson provides information on Evaluation Area 3, Protective Action Implementation.

Lesson Objectives

At the completion of this lesson, you will be able to:

- Identify the six elements to be evaluated under protective action implementation.
- Summarize the criteria used to evaluate protective action implementation.

OVERVIEW OF EVALUATION AREA 3

EA-3, Protective Action Implementation, includes 6 sub-elements:

3.a Implementation of Emergency Worker Exposure Control

3.b Implementation of KI Decision

3.c Implementation of Protective Actions for Special Populations

3.d Implementation of Traffic and Access Control

3.e Implementation of Ingestion Pathway Decisions

3.f Implementation of Relocation, Re-entry, and Return Decisions

Evaluation Frequency

The minimum frequency for evaluating these sub-elements is shown below:

Sub-Elements	Every Exercise	Once in 6 Years
3.a Emergency Worker Exposure Control 3.b KI Decision 3.c Protective Actions for Special Populations 3.d Traffic and Access Control 3.e Ingestion Pathway Decisions 3.f Relocation, Reentry, and Return	X X	X* X X X

* 3.b should be demonstrated in every biennial exercise by some OROs, and at least once every 6 years by every ORO with responsibility for implementing KI decisions.

3.a Emergency Worker Exposure Control

Sub-element 3.a, Implementation of Emergency Worker Exposure Control, assesses the ORO's ability to implement protective actions for emergency workers through the provision of dosimetry, maintenance of exposure records, and control of radiation exposures. It includes one criterion:

Criterion 3.a.1: The OROs issue appropriate dosimetry and procedures, and manage radiological exposure to emergency workers in accordance with the plans and procedures. Emergency workers periodically and at the end of each mission read their dosimeters and record the readings on the appropriate exposure record or chart.

Provision of Dosimetry

OROs should demonstrate the capability to provide emergency workers with appropriate dosimetry, including:

- Direct-reading dosimetry (DRD) and permanent record dosimetry (e.g., Thermo-Luminescence Dosimeter (TLD))
- Dosimeter chargers
- Instructions on the use of dosimetry

Appropriate DRD, for evaluation purposes, is dosimetry that allows individuals to read two limits contained in the ORO's plans/procedures: (1) administrative reporting limits (pre-established at a level low enough to consider subsequent calculation of Total Effective Dose Equivalent) and (2) maximum exposure limits (for emergency workers involved in life saving activities).

Although ideally every emergency worker should have a DRD, it may not always be strictly necessary. An example is when team members will be close to each other throughout the entire mission and one dosimeter worn by the team leader will be adequate for all team members.

Similarly, emergency workers assigned to low exposure rate areas (e.g., reception centers, counting laboratories, EOCs, and communications centers) may have individual DRDs or they may be monitored by dosimeters strategically placed in the work area.

Even in these situations, each team member must still have their own permanent record dosimetry.

What Is Required of the Emergency Worker?

Emergency workers should:

- Have basic knowledge of radiation exposure limits.
- Monitor and record dosimeter readings.
- Manage radiological exposure control.

During a plume phase exercise, they need to demonstrate the procedures for when administrative exposure limits and turn-back values are reached, and report accumulated exposures during the exercise.

If the scenario doesn't require authorizations for additional exposure, knowledge of the procedures will be checked through interviews with the workers. The workers may consult any available resources in responding.

3.b KI DECISION

Sub-element 3.b, Implementation of KI Decision, assesses the ORO's ability to provide radioprotective drugs for emergency workers, institutionalized individuals, and—if in the plan/procedures—the general public for whom immediate evacuation may be infeasible, very difficult, or significantly delayed. This sub-element contains one criterion:

Criterion 3.b.1: KI and appropriate instructions are available should a decision to recommend use of KI be made. Appropriate record keeping of the administration of KI for emergency workers and institutionalized individuals is maintained.

What the Policy Requires

The ORO's provisions for KI distribution should include:

- Availability of adequate quantities
- Storage
- Means of the distribution consistent with the decisions made.

While OROs must be able to provide KI to emergency workers and institutionalized individuals, providing KI to the general public is an ORO option that will be reflected in their plans and procedures. If a recommendation is made for the general public to take KI, appropriate information should be provided to the public by the means of notification specified in the ORO's plan and/or procedures.

Other requirements include:

- Disseminating instructions on the use of KI for those advised to take it.

- Maintaining lists of emergency workers and institutionalized individuals who have taken KI.
- Documentation of the date(s) and time(s) individuals were instructed to take KI.
- When the ORO health official recommends use of KI, taking it is voluntary. For evaluation purposes, the actual ingestion of KI is not necessary.

Emergency Workers

Emergency workers should demonstrate the basic knowledge of procedures for the use of KI. Demonstration of this knowledge is required whether or not the scenario actually calls for the use of KI and can be determined through an interview with the evaluator.

3.c SPECIAL POPULATIONS

Sub-element 3.c, Implementation of Protective Actions for Special Populations, assesses the ORO's ability to implement protective action decisions, including evacuation and/or sheltering, for all special populations. This sub-element includes two criteria:

Criterion 3.c.1: Protective action decisions are implemented for special

populations other than schools within areas subject to protective actions.

Criterion 3.c.2: OROs/School officials implement protective actions for schools.

3.c.1: Special Populations Other than Schools

Applicable OROs should demonstrate their ability to alert and notify special populations other than schools, such as:

- Hospitals and nursing homes
- Correctional facilities
- Mobility impaired individuals
- Transportation dependent

This might be done, for example, by providing protective action recommendations

(PARs) and emergency information and instructions to these groups.

Making Contact

OROs should also demonstrate their ability to provide for the needs of these special populations in accordance with the plan/procedures.

Contact with special populations and reception facilities may be actual or simulated, as agreed to in the Extent of Play.

Some contacts with transportation providers should be actual, as negotiated in the Extent of Play. All actual and simulated contacts should be logged.

3.c.2: Schools

School systems/districts (including all public schools, licensed day care centers, and participating private schools) must demonstrate the ability to implement protective actions for students, including developing and providing timely information to OROs for use in messages to parents, the general public, and the media on the status of protective actions for schools. Specifically:

- Protective actions need to be demonstrated by at least one school in each affected school system or district.
- School cancellation, early dismissal, and sheltering should be simulated by describing procedures to evaluators.
- For evacuation, activities may either be demonstrated or accomplished through an interview process.

At least one bus driver should be available to demonstrate knowledge of their role.

Routes can be run if negotiated and documented in the Extent of Play.

Evaluators should verify communications capabilities between school officials and the

buses, if required by the plan/procedures.

3.d TRAFFIC AND ACCESS CONTROL

Sub-element 3.d, Implementation of Traffic and Access Control, assesses the ORO's capability to implement protective action plans, including relocation and restriction of access to evacuated/sheltered areas. The focus is on selecting, establishing, and staffing of traffic and access control points and removal of impediments to the flow of evacuation traffic. Physical deployment of resources is not required. This sub-element includes two criteria:

3.d.1: Appropriate traffic and access control is established. Accurate instructions are provided to traffic and access control personnel.

3.d.2: Impediments to evacuation are identified and resolved.

3.d.1: Provisions for Traffic and Access Control

The ORO's provisions for traffic and access control should include:

- Selecting, establishing, and staffing appropriate traffic and access control points, consistent with protective action decisions (e.g., evacuating, sheltering, or relocation).
- Setting up traffic and access control in a timely manner. Instructing staff on what to do when changes in evacuation patterns or restricted area boundaries are necessary.

Job knowledge. Traffic and access control staff should demonstrate accurate knowledge of their roles and responsibilities. This may be done by actual deployment or by interview, in accordance with the Extent of Play agreement. If interviews are conducted, topics such as re-entry criteria, evacuation routes, and the location of reception centers or congregate care centers may be discussed.

Authority to control access. If the ORO lacks the authority to control access by certain types of traffic (rail, water, and air traffic), they should demonstrate the capability to contact the State or Federal agencies that do have authority to control access.

3.d.2: Impediments to Evacuation

OROs should demonstrate the capability, as required by the scenario, to identify and take appropriate actions concerning impediments to evacuation (e.g., debris, inoperable vehicles).

Actual dispatch of resources to deal with impediments, such as wreckers, need not be demonstrated. However, all contacts—actual or simulated—should be logged.

3.e INGESTION PATHWAY

Sub-element 3.e assesses the ORO's implementation of protective actions, based on criteria recommended by current FDA guidance, for the ingestion pathway zone (IPZ). The IPZ is the area within an approximate 50-mile radius of the nuclear power plant. Sub-element 2.e includes two criteria:

3.e.1: The ORO demonstrates the availability and appropriate use of adequate information regarding water, food supplies, milk, and agricultural production within the ingestion exposure pathway emergency planning zone for implementation of protective actions.

3.e.2: Appropriate measures, strategies, and pre-printed instructional material are developed for implementing protective action decisions for contaminated water, food products, milk, and agricultural production.

3.e.1: Information Availability

To implement protective actions within the IPZ, OROs need access to current

information on the locations of:

- Dairy farms
- Meat and poultry producers
- Fisheries
- Fruit and vegetable growers
- Grain producers
- Food processing plants
- Water supply intake points

To meet this criterion, OROs must show that they can obtain and use that information.

Use of Federal Resources

OROs should use Federal resources as identified in the Federal Radiological Emergency
Response Plan (FRERP), and other resources such as compacts and nuclear insurers if
available.

Evaluation of this criterion will take into consideration the level of Federal and other
resources participating in the exercise. The evaluator should read the specific Extent of
Play for the exercise and document the impact of Federal actions.

3.e.2: Measures and Strategies

OROs should demonstrate measures and strategies to implement IPZ protective actions.
This is can be done though provision of information, contamination control, and
communications and coordination.

- Information. The ORO needs to demonstrate that it is ready with protective action
  information for the general public and for food producers and processors. This
  can be demonstrated by having pre-distributed public information material in the
  IPZ or by having the ability to rapidly distribute pre-printed or camera-ready
  information and instructions to pre-determined individuals and businesses.
- Contamination control. OROs should demonstrate their ability to control, restrict,
  or prevent distribution of contaminated food by commercial sectors.
- Communication and coordination. During exercise play, communication and
  coordination should be evident between organizations to implement protective
  actions.

Actual field play of implementation activities may be simulated. For example,
communications and coordination with agencies responsible for enforcing food controls

within the IPZ should be demonstrated, but communications with food producers and processors may be simulated.

3.f RELOCATION, RE-ENTRY, AND RETURN

Sub-Element 3.f, Implementation of Relocation, Re-entry, and Return Decisions, assesses the ORO's ability to put decisions regarding relocation, re-entry, and return into action. This capability is essential for protecting the public from direct long-term exposure to deposited radioactive materials from a severe incident at a commercial nuclear power plant. This sub-element includes one criterion:

Criterion 3.f.1: Decisions regarding controlled re-entry of emergency workers and relocation and return of the public are coordinated with appropriate organizations and implemented.

Relocation

Key responsibilities related to relocation include:

- Coordinating and implementing decisions about relocation of individuals not previously evacuated to a safe area (i.e., where radiological contamination will not expose them to doses that exceed the relocation PAGs.).
    - o Providing for short- or long-term relocation of evacuees who lived in areas that have residual radiation levels above the PAGs.
    - o Of particular interest is the ability to communicate with OROs regarding:
- Timing of actions
- Procedures for relocation
- Notification of, and advice for, evacuated individuals who will be converted to relocation status.

OROs should also demonstrate their ability to communicate instructions to the public

regarding relocation decisions.

Re-Entry

Key areas related to implementation of re-entry decisions include:

- Controlling the re-entry and exit of individuals who temporarily re-enter the restricted area, to protect them from unnecessary radiation exposure.
- Controlling the exit of vehicles and other equipment, to control the spread of contamination outside the restricted area.
    - o Establishing monitoring and decontamination facilities.
    - o Several examples of control procedure decisions were discussed in Lesson 5. Briefly, they involved:

- Dosimetry for emergency workers
- Questioning of individuals wishing to enter the area
- Maps and plots of radiation exposure rates
- Advice on areas to avoid
- Exit procedures (e.g., monitoring of individuals, vehicles, and equipment; decision criteria regarding contamination; proper disposition of emergency worker dosimetry; and maintenance of emergency worker radiation exposure records)

These are the kinds of re-entry decisions whose implementation is evaluated under this criterion.

Return

OROs should demonstrate the capability to implement policies concerning return of members of the public to areas that were evacuated during the plume phase. This includes:

- Identifying and prioritizing services and facilities that require restoration within a few days, such as medical and social services, utilities, roads, schools, and intermediate-term housing for relocated persons.
- Identifying the procedures and resources for their restoration.

Other Exercise Concerns

Other concerns related to relocation, re-entry, and return include communications and

use of Federal resources.

- Communications. Communications among OROs for relocation, re-entry, and return may be simulated; however all simulated or actual contacts should be documented. These discussions may be accomplished in a group setting.
- Federal resources. OROs should use Federal resources as identified in the FRERP, and other resources (e.g., compacts, nuclear insurers), if available. Evaluation of this criterion will take into consideration the level of Federal and other resources participating in the exercise.

Lesson 7: EA-4—Field Measurement and Analysis

LESSON OVERVIEW

This lesson provides information on Evaluation Area 4, Field Measurement and

Analysis.

Lesson Objectives

At the completion of this lesson, you will be able to:

- Identify the three elements to be evaluated under field measurement and analysis.
- Summarize the criteria used to evaluate field measurement and analysis.

OVERVIEW OF EVALUATION AREA 4

Evaluation Area 4, Field Measurement and Analysis, includes three sub-elements:

4.a Plume Phase Field Measurements and Analysis

4.b Post-Plume Phase Field Measurements and Sampling

4.c Laboratory Operations

Evaluation Frequency

The minimum frequency for evaluating the criteria under these sub-elements is as
follows:

Sub-Elements	Minimum Frequency
4.a Plume Phase Field Measurements and Analysis	Every full-participation exercise
4.b Post-Plume Phase Field Measurements and Sampling 4.c Laboratory Operations	Once in 6 years

4.a PLUME PHASE

In the event of a nuclear power plant incident, the possible release of radioactive material
may pose a risk to the nearby population and environment. Although accident assessment

methods are available to project the extent and magnitude of a release, these methods are subject to large uncertainties.

During an incident, it is important to collect field radiological data to help characterize any radiological release. Adequate equipment and procedures are essential to such field measurement efforts.

Sub-element 4.a, Plume Phase Field Measurements and Analysis, assesses the ORO's capability to deploy field teams to perform those measurements. It includes three criteria:

Criterion 4.a.1: The field teams are equipped to perform field measurements of direct radiation exposure (cloud and ground shine) and to sample airborne radioiodine and particulates.

Criterion 4.a.2: Field teams are managed to obtain sufficient information to help characterize the release and to control radiation exposure.

Criterion 4.a.3: Ambient radiation measurements are made and recorded at appropriate locations, and radioiodine and particulate samples are collected. Teams will move to an appropriate low background location to determine whether any significant (as specified in the plan and/or procedures) amount of radioactivity has been collected on the sampling media.

4.a.1 Field Team Equipment

Field teams should be equipped with all instrumentation and supplies necessary to accomplish their mission. The instruments must be capable of:

- Measuring gamma exposure rates.
- Detecting the presence of beta radiation.
- Measuring a range of activity and exposure consistent with the intended use of the instrument and the ORO's plans and procedures.

Maintenance and Operability. All instruments should be operated, maintained, and calibrated in accordance with the manufacturer's recommendations. OROs should demonstrate verification of proper operational response for each instrument, according to specified standards.

4.a.2 Field Team Management

Criterion 4.a.2 requires that field teams be "managed to obtain sufficient information to help characterize the release and to control radiation exposure." OROs should demonstrate the capability to brief teams before deployment on predicted plume location and direction, travel speed, and exposure control procedures.

Field measurements are needed to help characterize the release and to support the implementation or modification of protective actions. Teams should be directed to take measurements at such times and locations that the needed information can be obtained.

Responsibility. If licensee field monitoring teams have accepted the responsibility to obtain peak measurements in the plume, with concurrence from OROs, State and local monitoring teams do not have to repeat these measurements. If the licensee teams do not obtain such measurements, it is the ORO's decision as to whether peak measurements are necessary to sufficiently characterize the plume.

Coordination. The sharing and coordination of plume measurement information among all field teams (licensee, Federal, and ORO) is essential. Coordination concerning transfer of samples, including a chain-of-custody form, to a radiological laboratory should be demonstrated.

OROs should use Federal and other resources if available. Evaluation of this criterion will take into consideration the level of Federal and other resources participating in the exercise.

4.a.3 Taking and Reporting Measurements

Criterion 4.a.3 focuses on the actual taking and reporting of measurements. It requires that "ambient radiation measurements are made and recorded at appropriate locations, and radioiodine and particulate samples are collected. Teams will move to an appropriate low background location to determine whether any significant (as specified in the plan and/or procedures) amount of radioactivity has been collected on the sampling media." The ORO must:

- Demonstrate the capability to take and report measurements and field data.
- Consider the need for expedited lab analysis for samples significantly above background levels.
    - Share data in a timely manner with other OROs.
    - Methodology. The ORO's methodology must be in accordance with the ORO's plan and/or procedures. This applies to:
- Contamination control
- Instrumentation
- Preparation of samples
- Chain-of-custody form for transfer to a laboratory

4.b POST-PLUME PHASE

Sub-element 4.b, Post-Plume Phase Field Measurements and Sampling, evaluates the capability to assess the actual or potential magnitude and locations of radiological hazards in the ingestion pathway zone (IPZ).

This sub-element focuses on the collection of environmental samples for laboratory analyses that are essential for decisions on protection of the public from contaminated food and water and direct radiation from deposited materials, and for relocation, reentry and return measures. This sub-element has one criterion:

Criterion 4.b.1: The field teams demonstrate the capability to make appropriate measurements and to collect appropriate samples (for example, food crops, milk, water, vegetation, and soil) to support adequate assessments and protective action decision-making.

Measurements and Samples. To meet this criterion, the ORO's field team should demonstrate the capability to take measurements and samples, at such times and locations as directed, to enable an adequate assessment of the ingestion pathway and to support re-entry, relocation, and return decisions.

When resources are available, the use of aerial surveys and in-situ gamma

measurement is appropriate.

Methodology and Sources. All methodology is to be in accordance with the ORO's plan and/or procedures. This includes methodology for contamination control, Instrumentation, preparation of samples, and chain-of-custody in transferring samples to a laboratory. Samples should be taken from appropriate sources:

- Ingestion pathway samples should be taken from agricultural products and water.
- Samples in support of relocation and return should be secured from soil, vegetation, and other surfaces in areas that received radioactive ground deposition.

Federal Resources. OROs should use Federal resources (e.g., DOE, EPA) and other resources if available. Evaluation of this criterion will take into consideration the level of Federal and other resources participating in the exercise. Links to Federal websites are provided at the end of this lesson.

4.c LABORATORY OPERATIONS

Sub-element 4.c, Laboratory Operations, assesses the capability to perform laboratory analyses of radioactivity in air, liquid, and environmental samples to support protective action decision-making. This sub-element includes one criterion:

Criterion 4.c.1: The laboratory is capable of performing required radiological

analyses to support protective action decisions.

Staff Capability. The laboratory staff should demonstrate appropriate procedures for:

- Receiving samples
- Preparing samples for conducting measurements
- Contamination control
  - Radioanalytical techniques
  - Specific procedures to be demonstrated include:
- Logging of information
- Preventing contamination of the laboratory
- Preventing buildup of background radiation due to stored samples
- Preventing cross-contamination of samples
- Preserving samples that may spoil (for example, milk)
- Keeping track of sample identity

Laboratory Equipment. The laboratory should be appropriately equipped to provide

analyses of media:

- As requested.
- On a timely basis.
- Of sufficient quality and sensitivity to support assessments and decisions as anticipated by the ORO's plans and procedures.

Instrument calibrations should meet specified standards.

Laboratory Methods. In analyzing typical radionuclides released in a reactor

incident, the laboratory methods should be as described in the plans and procedures.

In analyzing atypical radionuclide releases (for example, transuranics or those resulting from a terrorist event), or when warranted by circumstances of the event, new or revised laboratory methods may be used. Analysis may require resources beyond those of the ORO.

Federal Resources. OROs should use Federal and other resources if available. Evaluation of this criterion will take into consideration the level of Federal and other resources participating in the exercise.

Lesson 8: EA-5—Emergency Notification & Public Information

This lesson provides information on Evaluation Area 5, Emergency Notification and

Public Information.

Lesson Objectives

At the completion of this lesson, you will be able to:

- Identify the two elements to be evaluated under emergency notification and public information.
- Summarize the criteria used to evaluate emergency notification and public information.

OVERVIEW OF EVALUATION AREA 5

EA-5, Emergency Notification and Public Information, looks at the ORO's ability to notify the public of an incident and to effectively communicate protective action decisions. It includes two sub-elements:

5.a Activation of the Prompt Alert and Notification System

5.b Emergency Information and Instructions for the Public and Media

5.a ALERT AND NOTIFICATION

Sub-element 5.a, Activation of the Prompt Alert and Notification (A&N) System, assesses the ORO's ability to provide prompt instructions to the public within the plume pathway EPZ. Two criteria have been published; a third has been deferred for later publication.

Criterion Concerns . . .

5.a.1	Timeliness and quality of primary alert and notification
5.a.2	[Alert and notification in "fast-breaker" situations–Deferred]
5.a.3	Backup alerting and notification and exception areas

These criteria are to be evaluated every exercise (5.a.3 every exercise as needed).

Alert vs. Notification

- Alert refers to activation of an attention-getting warning signal (e.g., by sirens, tone alert radio, TDD, EAS, route alerting, or speakers on cars, helicopters, or boats) to alert the public to the emergency.
- Notification refers to distribution of an instructional message through the Emergency Alert System (EAS) or some other system.

Criterion 5.a.1: Primary Alerting and Notification

This criterion states: Activities associated with primary alerting and notification of the public are completed in a timely manner following the initial decision by authorized offsite emergency officials to notify the public of an emergency situation. The initial instructional message to the public must include as a minimum the elements required by current FEMA REP guidance.

Meeting the 5.a.1 Criterion

5.a.1 has several components. The ORO should demonstrate the capability to:

- Sequentially provide an alert signal followed by an initial instructional message.
- Provide the signal and message to populated areas throughout the 10-mile plume pathway EPZ.
- Complete the A&N in a timely manner.
- Include the elements required by current FEMA REP guidance in the initial message.

"Timely manner" is not subject to specific time requirements. It will be judged in relation to the scenario. For exercise purposes, this definition is used:

Timely: The responsible ORO personnel/representatives demonstrate actions to disseminate the appropriate information/instructions with a sense of urgency and without undue delay.

If message dissemination is to be identified as not having been accomplished in a timely manner, evaluators need to document a specific delay or cause as to why a message was not considered timely. Be sure to record times and document circumstances!

Required Message Elements. The required content of initial EAS messages depends on the emergency. Current FEMA REP guidance requires that messages contain, as a minimum, these four components:

- Identification of the ORO and the official authorizing the A&N.
- Identification of the power station and a statement that an emergency exists at the plant.

- Reference to REP-specific emergency information (e.g., brochures, information in the phone book).
- Closing statement asking people to stay tuned.

Simulated vs. Actual. Procedures to broadcast the message should be fully demonstrated as they would in an actual emergency up to the point of transmission. Broadcast of the message(s) or test messages is not required.

The alert signal activation may be simulated. However, the procedures should be

demonstrated up to the point of actual activation.

The capability of the primary notification system to broadcast an instructional message on a 24-hour basis should be verified during an interview with appropriate personnel from the primary notification system.

Criterion 5.a.3: Exception Areas and Backup Alert

This criterion states: Activities associated with FEMA approved exception areas (where applicable) are completed within 45 minutes following the initial decision by authorized offsite emergency officials to notify the public of an emergency situation. Backup alert and notification of the public is completed within 45 minutes following the detection by the ORO of a failure of the primary alert and notification system.

An exception area is an area located about 5 to 10 miles from a nuclear power plant, specifically designated in an organization's plan, for which the 15-minute A&N provision does not apply.

Exception Area Alerting

OROs with FEMA-approved exception areas should be able to complete primary A&N of the exception area(s) within 45 minutes after the initial decision to notify the public, as follows:

Timing. The 45-minute clock will begin when the OROs make the decision to activate the A&N system for the first time for a specific emergency situation.

Message content. The initial message should, at a minimum, include:

- A statement that an emergency exists at the plant.
- Where to obtain additional information.

Routes. At least one route needs to be demonstrated and evaluated. The selected route(s) should vary from exercise to exercise, and the most difficult route should be demonstrated at least once every 6 years.

Simulation. All A&N activities along the route should be simulated as agreed upon in the Extent of Play. That is, the message that would actually be used is read for the evaluator, but not actually broadcast.

Actual testing. Actual testing of the mobile public address system will be conducted at some agreed-upon location.

Backup Alerting

Backup alert and notification of the public should be completed as follows:

Timing. Backup A&N should be completed within 45 minutes after the ORO detects a

failure of the primary A&N system.

Situation. Backup route alerting needs to be demonstrated and evaluated (per the

ORO's plan/procedures and the Extent of Play agreement) only if:

- The exercise scenario calls for failure of any portion of the primary system(s).
    - Any portion of the primary system(s) actually fails to function.
    - Implementation. If backup alerting is demonstrated:
- Only one route needs to be selected and demonstrated.
- All alert and notification activities along the route should be simulated as agreed upon in the Extent of Play.
- Actual testing of the mobile public address system will be conducted at some agreed-upon location.

5.b EMERGENCY INFORMATION

Sub-element 5.b, Emergency Information and Instructions for the Public and the Media, assesses the ORO's ability to disseminate emergency information and instructions to the public and the media and to maintain a public inquiry hotline.

This sub-element includes one criterion:

Criterion 5.b.1: OROs provide accurate emergency information and instructions to the public and the news media in a timely manner.

Timely and Sufficient Information

After the A&N has been accomplished, subsequent emergency information and instructions should be provided to the public and the media in a timely manner. Again, timeliness is scenario-dependent, and a determination that timeliness has been inadequate must be documented and justified.

Emergency information and instructions should be consistent with protective action decisions made by appropriate officials. They should contain sufficient instructions to assist the public in carrying out the protective actions. Examples of information to be provided are listed on the next screen.

Types of Information Provided

Examples of information provided to the public include:

- Evacuation instructions
- Evacuation routes
- Reception center locations
- What to take when evacuating
- Information concerning pets
- Shelter-in-place instructions
- Information concerning protective actions for schools and special populations
- Public inquiry telephone number

Information Clarity

Key aspects of effectively communicating with the public and media include:

- Disclosing and explaining the incident ECL. (At a minimum, the ECL must be included in media briefings and for media releases.)
- Using language that is clear and understandable to the public within both the plume and ingestion pathway EPZs.
- Using familiar landmarks and boundaries to describe protective action areas.
- Developing emergency information in a non-English language when required by the plan and/or procedures.

Quality of Information

OROs need to ensure that information provided the public and media is:

- All-inclusive: Previously identified protective action areas that are still valid are included along with new areas.
- Up-to-date: Information that is no longer valid is rescinded and not repeated by broadcast media.
- Repeated regularly: Current emergency information is repeated at preestablished intervals in accordance with the plan and/or procedures.

Information on Ingestion Pathway Measures

If ingestion pathway measures are used, OROs should have a system in place for rapid dissemination of ingestion pathway information to pre-determined individuals and businesses.

Information for the Media

OROs should be able to provide information to the news media for subsequent

dissemination to the public. This should include:

- Providing accurate, concise, and coordinated information.
- Conducting timely and pertinent media briefings.
- Distributing media releases as the situation warrants.
- Responding appropriately to inquiries from the news media.
- Making copies of pertinent emergency information (e.g., EAS messages and media releases) and media information kits available for dissemination to the media.

All information presented in media briefings and media releases should be consistent with protective action decisions and other emergency information provided to the public.

Public Inquiry Hotline

OROs should have an effective system in place for dealing with calls to the public inquiry hotline. This should include:

- Having hotline staff who are capable of providing or obtaining accurate information for callers or referring them to an appropriate information source.
- Including information from the hotline staff (including information that corrects false or inaccurate information when trends are noted) in emergency information provided to the public, media briefings, and/or media releases.

Lesson 9: EA-6—Support Operations/Facilities

LESSON OVERVIEW

This lesson provides information on Evaluation Area 6, Support Operations/Facilities.

Lesson Objectives

At the completion of this lesson, you will be able to:

- Identify the four elements to be evaluated under support operations and facilities.
- Summarize the criteria used to evaluate support operations and facilities issues immediately.

OVERVIEW OF EVALUATION AREA 6

EA-6, Support Operations/Facilities, assesses the ORO's ability to account for, monitor, and decontaminate evacuees, emergency workers, and emergency worker equipment; to provide temporary care of evacuees; and to ensure that capabilities exist for transporting and treating injured individuals who have been exposed to radiation. The area is divided into four sub-elements:

a. Monitoring and Decontamination of Evacuees and Emergency Workers and Registration of Evacuees
b. Monitoring and Decontamination of Emergency Worker Equipment
c. Temporary Care of Evacuees
d. Transportation and Treatment of Contaminated Individuals

Evaluation Frequency

The minimum frequency for evaluating criteria under these sub-elements is shown in the table below.

Sub-Elements	Minimum Frequency
6.a & 6.b Monitoring & Decontamination	Every facility once in 6 years.
6.c Temporary Care	ARC-managed facilities: After baseline–when newly designated or substantially changed. Non-ARC-managed facilities: Evaluated once in 6 years.
6.d Transportation & Treatment	Every 2 years.

6.a MONITORING, DECONTAMINATION, REGISTRATION

Sub-element 6.a looks at the ORO's capability to implement radiological monitoring and decontamination of evacuees and emergency workers, while minimizing contamination of the facility, and registration of evacuees at reception centers. It includes one criterion:

6.a.1: The reception center/emergency worker facility has appropriate space, adequate resources, and trained personnel to provide monitoring, decontamination, and registration of evacuees and/or emergency workers.

Reception Center Facilities

Radiological monitoring, decontamination, and registration facilities for evacuees/emergency workers should be set up and demonstrated as they would be in an actual emergency or as indicated in the extent of play agreement. Adequate space for evacuees' vehicles should be demonstrated.

Scope of the Demonstration

The ORO's demonstration should include one-third of the monitoring teams/portal monitors required to monitor 20 percent of the population allocated to the facility within 12 hours. (This will be worked out in advance by the Region in the Extent of Play.)

The process of operationally checking the instrument(s) should be demonstrated before instrument use begins.

Monitoring Capacity

Evacuees. Monitoring staff should demonstrate the capability to attain and sustain a monitoring productivity rate per hour needed to monitor the 20 percent EPZ population-planning base within about 12 hours. Monitoring productivity rate per hour is the number of evacuees that can be monitored per hour by the total complement of monitors using an appropriate monitoring procedure.

At least six individuals per monitoring station should be monitored, to allow demonstration of monitoring, decontamination, and registration capabilities. Individuals can be used more than once as simulated evacuees.

Evaluators will time the monitoring sequences for the first six simulated evacuees per team to determine whether the 12-hour requirement can be met.

Emergency Workers. Monitoring of emergency workers does not have to meet the 12-hour requirement. However, appropriate monitoring procedures should be demonstrated for at least two emergency workers.

Decontamination

Decontamination of evacuees/emergency workers may be simulated and conducted by interview. Demonstrations should include the ORO's provisions for:

- Separate male/female showering arrangements.
- Limiting the spread of contamination (e.g., using floor coverings, signs, partitions, and roped-off areas).
- Separating contaminated and uncontaminated individuals.
- Providing changes of clothing and storing contaminated clothing and personal belongings.
- Handling the potential contamination of vehicles and personal belongings by contaminated evacuees.

Decisionmaking and Referrals

Monitoring personnel should explain:

- Use of action levels for determining the need for decontamination.
- Procedures for referring evacuees who cannot be adequately decontaminated for assessment and followup.

Contamination of the individual will be determined by controller inject and not simulated with any low-level radiation source.

Registration

The ORO should demonstrate the capability to register individuals after monitoring and decontamination, including development of a registration record for each individual. Registration can be completed via audio recorders, camcorders, or written records.

Review

Based on the general Extent of Play, the table below summarizes how each aspect of reception center monitoring is to be handled in the exercise evaluation. Evaluators need to know their region's specific exercise Extent of Play to determine what will be actual or simulated.

Can Be Simulated and Discussed

• Decontamination of evacuees • Decontamination of emergency workers • Decontamination of evacuee vehicles • Decisionmaking and referrals

Must Be Demonstrated

• Physical setup • Limiting spread of contamination • Registration • Monitoring 6 evacuees • Monitoring 2 emergency workers

6.b EQUIPMENT DECONTAMINATION

Sub-element 6.b, Monitoring and Decontamination of Emergency Worker Equipment, assesses the ORO's capability to implement radiological monitoring and decontamination of emergency worker equipment, including vehicles. It includes one criterion:

6.b.1: The facility/ORO has adequate procedures and resources for the accomplishment of monitoring and decontamination of emergency worker equipment, including vehicles.

Monitoring of Equipment

The ORO should demonstrate the ability to:

- Monitor equipment, including vehicles, for contamination, giving specific attention given to equipment that was in contact with contaminated individuals.
- Make decisions on the need for decontamination based on guidance levels and procedures stated in the plan and/or procedures.

The monitoring and decontamination area should be set up as in an actual emergency, with all route markings, instrumentation, record keeping, and contamination control measures in place.

Monitoring Procedures

Monitoring procedures should be demonstrated for a minimum of one vehicle, including radiator grills, bumpers, wheel wells, tires, door, and interior surfaces of vehicles that were in contact with contaminated individuals. It is generally not necessary to monitor the entire vehicle surface.

Equipment Decontamination

Decontamination capabilities, and provisions for vehicles and equipment that cannot be decontaminated, may be simulated and conducted by interview.

Evaluators should make note of combined facilities for monitoring evacuees and emergency workers at the same location.

6.c TEMPORARY CARE

Sub-element 6.c, Temporary Care of Evacuees, assesses the ORO's capability to establish relocation centers in host areas. The American Red Cross (ARC) normally provides congregate care in support of OROs under existing letters of agreement. Sub-element 6.c includes one criterion:

6.c.1: Managers of congregate care facilities demonstrate that the centers have resources to provide services and accommodations consistent with ARC planning guidelines. (Found in MASS CARE–Preparedness Operations, ARC 3031). Managers demonstrate the procedures to assure that evacuees have been monitored for contamination and have been decontaminated as appropriate before entering congregate care facilities.

Frequency. Facilities managed by the American Red Cross (ARC), under the ARC/FEMA Memorandum of Understanding, will be evaluated once when designated or when substantial changes occur. All other facilities not managed by the ARC must be evaluated once in the 6-year exercise cycle.

Evaluation of Congregate Care Centers

Congregate care centers can be evaluated through simulation or demonstration.

- Simulation. Demonstration of congregate care centers may be conducted out of sequence with the exercise scenario. It is not necessary to set up operations as they would be in an actual emergency. The evaluator should conduct a walkthrough of the center to determine, through observation and inquiries, that services and accommodations are consistent with ARC 3031.
- Demonstration. Alternatively, capabilities may be demonstrated by setting up stations for various services and providing those services to simulated evacuees.

Given the substantial differences between demonstration and simulation of this objective, exercise demonstration expectations should be clearly specified in Extent of Play agreements.

Services to Evacuees

Congregate care staff should also demonstrate the capability to ensure that evacuees have been:

- Monitored for contamination.
- Decontaminated as appropriate.
- Registered before entering the facility. This capability may be determined through an interview process.

Availability of Equipment and Supplies

If operations at the center are demonstrated, material that would be difficult or expensive to transport (for example, cots, blankets, sundries, and large-scale food supplies) need not be physically available at the facility.

Availability of such items should be verified by providing the evaluator a list of sources with locations and estimates of quantities.

6.d TRANSPORTATION AND TREATMENT

Sub-element 6.d, Transportation and Treatment of Contaminated Individuals, assesses the ORO's capability to transport contaminated injured individuals to medical facilities. This sub-element contains one criterion:

6.d.1 The facility/ORO has the appropriate space, adequate resources, and trained personnel to provide transport, monitoring, decontamination, and medical services to contaminated injured individuals.

Note: Evaluators should not focus on the medical treatment of the victims. Radiological aspects of the situation are your primary concern.

Victim Transport

Monitoring, decontamination, and contamination control efforts must not delay urgent medical care for the victim. The ORO should demonstrate the ability to transport contaminated injured individuals to medical facilities. Performance criteria relate to type of vehicle, en route communications, and staff awareness.

- Type of vehicle. An ambulance should be used for the response to the victim. However, to avoid taking an ambulance out of service for an extended time, any vehicle (e.g., car, truck, or van) may be used to transport the victim to the medical facility.
- Communications. Normal communications between the ambulance/dispatcher and the receiving medical facility should be demonstrated and should include reporting radiation monitoring results, if available. If a substitute vehicle is used, this communication must occur before releasing the ambulance from the drill.
- Staff awareness. The ambulance crew should demonstrate, by interview, knowledge of where the ambulance and crew would be monitored and decontaminated, if required, or whom to contact for such information.

Victim Monitoring

All monitoring activities should be completed as they would be in an actual emergency. The victim may be monitored before transport, en route, or deferred to the medical facility.

Before using monitoring instruments, staff should demonstrate operational checks of the instruments. Contamination control measures should be demonstrated before and during transport and at the receiving medical facility.

At the Medical Facility

The medical facility should demonstrate the capability to activate and set up a radiological emergency area for treatment, with equipment and supplies available for treating contaminated injured individuals. The medical facility should demonstrate its ability to:

- Make decisions on the need for decontamination of the individual.
- Follow appropriate decontamination procedures.
- Maintain records of all survey measurements and samples taken.

Procedures for sample collection and analysis and for decontamination of individuals should be demonstrated or described to the evaluator.